BLACK

IN

BLUE

BLACK

IN

BLUE

A

study

of

the

Negro

policeman

Nicholas Alex

HERBERT H. LEHMAN COLLEGE
THE CITY UNIVERSITY OF NEW YORK

APPLETON-CENTURY-CROFTS
Educational Division
New York   MEREDITH CORPORATION

To my wife, Deanne

PREFACE

IN THIS book I have made an effort to examine the peculiar problems of Negro policemen who live in an age which has not yet resolved the problem of inequality in an assertedly democratic society. In doing so I have drawn heavily on the reflections of forty-one Negro policemen who made plain to me the difficulties involved in being black and blue.

I was concerned in this study with the ways in which these men were recruited into the police, the nature of their relations in regard to their immediate clientele, their white counterparts, and the rest of society, and the consequences of their actions as they saw them. In broadest terms, then, my book examines the special problems that Negro policemen face in their efforts to reconcile their race with their work in the present framework of American values and beliefs.

The research for the study was based on intensive interviews collected over a period of eleven months, from December 1964 to October 1965. During that time I talked with Negro policemen engaged in different types of police specialties, men of different rank and backgrounds; but now, in the interest of preserving their anonymity, I have substituted code numbers for names. The language in which their thoughts were expressed is, as the reader may notice, unchanged.

While most of my interviews were obtained either at the policeman's home or mine, some transpired in parks, playgrounds, and luncheonettes. They were informal and open-ended; that is, while my questions were specific, I tried to give my respondents the latitude for free and spontaneous expression of thoughts and feelings which would be important to an understanding of their work lives. Interestingly enough, all refused to have our conversations recorded on tape. "I know too well what tapes can do to you," said one. "I can refute what you write down on that pad, but I can't if it's taped. We use tapes too, you know."

It should be stressed that the forty-one interviews are in no way meant to be a representative sample of the estimated 1,500 Negro policemen who work for the department. The administrative framework which would provide a basis for such sampling was not available to me. A practical alternative was to use the "snowball" technique in finding policemen. This technique simply consisted of finding one or more policemen and asking them if they knew of friends, associates, or acquaintances to be interviewed. This resulted in a "chain letter" of contacts and subsequent interviews. It is perhaps ironical from the standpoint of my present study, that the snowball technique was originally devised by the police in an attempt to locate criminals.

I was not dependent, however, on any one original source as the starting point for seeking out policemen. By using a wide variety and number of starting points, I attempted to secure as representative a group as possible, given the absence of data and administrative means which would have allowed me adequate representation. Starting points included seven nonpolice contact sources, eight police sources known to me, and eleven police sources unknown to me at the outset.

Forty-eight policemen were contacted through these three sources, but, as I have indicated, only forty-one were subsequently interviewed. Those not interviewed either refused to be interviewed or couldn't be reached after they had initially agreed to "testify." All of the forty-one policemen interviewed were not self-selected, nor did they volunteer. And many of them were not necessarily "willing." Many had to be convinced of the worthiness of being interviewed.

I hope the reader will judge this study on the merits and authenticity of the data. As my field work progressed I became increasingly aware that I was dealing with a highly expressive and literate group of men who thought of my study as a way in which they could make themselves heard. Being a black policeman seems to cultivate a high degree of self-awareness, sensitivity, and self-consciousness. Sociologists have known for a long time that it is just this type of informant who provides the researcher with a perspective on society that truly reflects a sociological attitude. Because of his multi-faceted marginality, the Negro policeman ironically seems to be in a position to see American society with a quality of detachment ordinarily more characteristic of the alien.

Finally, I had originally intended to mask the identity of the department itself, but since the problems I deal with are most often seen in a metropolitan setting and indeed are exacerbated by it, I think it would serve no useful purpose, and in fact might in the long run be damaging to the tradition of sociological research, if I were to conceal the fact that the Negro policemen discussed in this study are employed by the City of New York.

Many people have helped me in the course of my work on this book. More than anyone else, I am indebted to Joseph Bensman, who, in addition to his time, offered important critical and constructive criticisms. I wish to express my thanks to Arthur J. Vidich for advice and editorial aid at several stages.

I am grateful to Irving Torgoff for having suggested the study, and for providing me with a most intriguing view of the problem. Gerald Levy's enthusiasm for the study as well as his personal counsel was a constant source of support. I owe thanks to Murray Hausknecht whose judicious comments were of great value to me.

For help in the initial stages of the research, I must thank Harry Silverstein. I owe a special thanks to Lloyd Douglas for his help in conducting several pilot interviews. I wish to express my appreciation also to Hubert O'Gorman, Alphonso Pinkney, Dan Waldorf, Margaret Donnelly, Mary Gardner, Constance Poster, Eugene Callender, Walter Christmas, and Bernard Rosenberg, to whom I turned for special advice and information. I wish to thank Shirley Lerman for the care which she gave to the typing of the manuscript.

To my wife, Deanne Alex, for her continued interest in my

work, and for her encouragement and support, I owe my loving thanks.

And lastly, I must acknowledge my great debt to those police-men who made this study possible. I regret that I cannot thank them here individually.

N. A.

FOREWORD

DURING most of the 1968 presidential campaign, the issue of "law and order" and "crime in the streets" was perhaps the second, if not the most important issue in that campaign. A proponent of "law and order," of course, won that election, and a majority of the total American electorate voted for presidential candidates who campaigned on that issue. Although it is possible to say that much of Nixon's election was a product of disenchantment with the Johnson regime, including President Johnson's failure to either win the war in Vietnam or to make peace by negotiation, it is just as easily said that a great many of those who ultimately voted for Hubert H. Humphrey did so in spite of strong response to the law and order issue as defined by his rivals.

It will take years before the full implications of the election are analyzed and understood. It is clear, however, that "law and order" was not only a major issue in that election, but also that that concern over the issue may have been even stronger in the minds and emotions of both white and black Americans than the election returns revealed. This is to say that issues of peace in Vietnam (the bombing halt) and of trade-unionist social legislation diluted the strength of the law and order issue. Moreover, that issue is likely to remain a basic political, social, and racial issue in American society in both the near and distant future. It is clear to me that the situations that call forth the issue will remain with us for a long time to come. The election of a proponent of "law and order" will not, in itself, resolve these conditions. For the issue of law and order involves deep and historic conflicts in the meaning, emotions, loyalties, and institutions that are at the very roots of American society.

Above all, the phrase "law and order" and "violence in the

streets" are ambiguous terms, code words that conceal pressures and movements that are too frightful to contemplate openly. Yet they are code words that all parties to the discussion understand both in their public "screen" meanings and in the actual intended meaning. As a result there is a multiplicity of meanings which are a function of both political and racial commitments of the users of these terms and of their choice to speak either openly or indirectly on the troubling issues of race in America.

The phrase "law and order" refers, in the context of contemporary American society, to policies that governmental bodies can take to curtail the black revolution. It refers to the role of the police, the courts, the state militia, and the National Guard in policing the blacks and in repressing civil-rights demonstrations, race riots, and "crime in the streets." To a lesser extent it refers to the role of police in the repression of student radicals in their attempts to take over, reform, or "destroy" our universities, and of Yippies in their attempts to provoke the "pigs" into showing their "true colors."

The advocates of law and order thus commit themselves to repression of movements from the "left," though the word "left" at present bears little relationship to traditional definitions of the term. "Law and order" implies the protection of life and property, but it bears overtones of racism on the part of a large number of whites—those who now feel, no matter how recently they have acquired it, that they have a stake in American society by virtue of thirty years of prosperity, by virtue of owning a home and an automobile and having a relatively well-paying job that is protected by seniority and tenure. The advocates and supporters of law and order include southern whites at all occupational and income levels who see the mobility and new political aggressiveness of the blacks as a threat to their racial dominance over their society. They include blue-collar workers, especially union members in the North, who by virtue of their union membership and prosperity have discovered that they have "arrived." They have achieved far more than they could have imagined at the outset of their careers. It especially includes older immigrants who have "made it" and who now consider themselves full-fledged Americans. They thus object intensely to those who have not yet made it—American blacks—and to those (i.e., middle-class radical students) who have, but who do not appreciate it.

The supporters of law and order include members of the old middle classes, the shopkeepers and their white employees who have been threatened physically or who can see themselves threatened by race riots, demonstrations, and violent crime. They include blue-collar workers, white-collar workers, and professionals whose jobs are directly threatened by job mobility among the blacks and by the easing of contractual and de facto job discrimination. White urbanites, living on the fringes or in the path of growing, moving black ghettoes, hope that by "law and order" ways may be found to contain the ghetto and prevent it from contaminating their living space.

In short, the last twenty years has seen the emergence of a new petite bourgeoisie, deriving from many sources, with a stake in American society, with property, established job rights, and a new respectability. This new petite bourgeoisie looks to the police, political leaders, bosses, and potential leaders to protect them from being deluged by the increasingly self-conscious, aggressive, militant, and, at times, violent black masses and by white radical students.

But "law and order" means different things—and yet the same thing—to an as yet undetermined number of the "black masses." It means historically, as Nicholas Alex demonstrates throughout this study, the use of sadistic red-neck cops in the South to keep blacks "in their place," to keep them segregated, discriminated against, exploited, and brutalized. To blacks it means police brutality, provocation, and the epitome of all that is repressive in the history and operation of American black-white relations.

A third group, consisting primarily of much maligned (by both sides) white liberals, doubts that such law and order will even be effective in its repression. They, as indicated by the Kerner report, see "white" law and order as provocative, as only an invitation to black lawlessness. In the light of the 1954 Supreme Court decisions and of the new hope engendered by that decision and the subsequent black civil-rights movement, police brutality, repression, and provocation is no longer tolerable to blacks. As a result, one of the major causes of urban race riots during the period from World War II to 1967 has been the overt and uncontrolled acts of police brutality directed against black suspects and offenders at times when racial tensions in urban ghettoes were already aroused.

Police brutality, sadism, and lack of self-control no longer "works" as it did in the past. Such brutality could only work as long as blacks were unorganized, as long as they felt hopeless, that what they had to lose was valuable. The hope evoked by the Supreme Court decisions and by the initial successes of the southern sit-ins and school and bus desegregation demonstrations has been dashed by the failure of subsequent demonstrations and federal poverty programs to produce substantial social and economic gains or opportunities. Black rage, and sense of outrage, has grown to such proportions that it is almost impossible to contain. Race riots, looting, and burning have been the answer that black youth have given to police brutality; and race riots have with few exceptions provoked repressive action by the police, by state militia, and by the National Guard. As a result, blacks have become more inflamed, have been driven to support more extreme anti-white racist leaders and programs. The new white petite bourgeoisie has been driven to support more extreme anti-black racists. The polarization of American society has proceeded so quickly that one despairs that anything but a totally repressive system of "law and order" can emerge. The danger is not the lawlessness, riots, and racial violence emerging from the sense of outrage among the blacks, but the repressive over-reaction of the emerging white petite bourgeoisie. Blacks represent approximately 10 percent of the American population, and only a small but highly visible part of these are aggressively militant. The new petite bourgeoisie, in its aggressive anti-black attitudes, may constitute the potential for a distinctly American form of racist-based fascism.

Historically, America has never lacked and at present does not lack leaders and would-be leaders willing to lead a crusade against blacks, against civil libertarians, and all those in American society who defend traditional liberal and civil-rights values. Such a crusade, in the light of current rhetorical styles, would be carried out under the banner of "law and order," a law and order that denies the protection of civil liberties and law under the Constitution.

It is doubtful that such a crusade can be directed only against the blacks. To achieve victory, as all history indicates, the intellectuals must be eliminated, the free press muzzled, the courts made first impotent and than an agency of repression. The churches, to the extent that they speak for the humanity of all men, must be silenced. While the blacks are the primary target of present movements to restore law and order, the success of such a crusade would be the destruction of traditional American democracy as we know it.

All of this seems far removed from the study of the *Black in Blue,* the black policeman in New York City. But it seems to me that in every period of historical crisis there are groups, occupations, and classes who are "accidentally" located in the "nutcrackers" of history. Such groups experience in extreme form all the cross-pressures, tensions, and contradictions of a society in the process of tearing itself apart. The intelligentsia in Russia at the eve and during the Russian Revolution was in such a nutcracker. The Russian intellectuals were forced to choose between the repressiveness of the past and the emerging and even greater repressiveness of the future; no matter which way they chose they were destroyed by the nut-cracker. The libertarian in the French Revolution and the democratic populist in the post-Civil War South were also in such nut-crackers.

In the current civil-rights crises there are large numbers of groups variously situated in the nut-crackers of history. White liberals who strive to keep an open dialogue between black and white and who contribute to programs or advocate actions that attempt to solve specific problems of poverty, discrimination, and educational and job opportunities of blacks increasingly alienate themselves from both whites and blacks as the polarization, extremism, and irrationality appear more and more to dominate public discussion on race issues. Black leaders who attempt to work out specific legislative programs for the solution of these problems face the same antagonism by the blacks, even while white opposition to these programs makes it almost impossible to secure their adoption. The attempt to do so evokes the epithet "Dr. Thomas" (an Uncle Tom with a Ph.D.), abuse, and threats from extremist and irrational blacks who have already repudiated all attempts to deal with specific problems short of taking over white society as it impinges on them.

In metropolitan areas, white liberal school teachers are in the same nut-cracker of history. For most of their lives they have prided themselves on their liberalism, their dedication to educating black children and to improving the lot of their pupils. But as the rage of the blacks has increased, they have found that their pupils have not responded to their efforts and that black parents have accused them of being middle-class racists, incapable of educating their children. Moreover, segments of the "black community" and white liberal politicians appear to be conspiring to deprive white teachers and school administrators of their jobs and promotions, insisting that less qualified (by established civil-service standards) black teachers and school administrators be given positions in their school systems. White educators are thus under pressure to renounce the liberalism by which they have defined themselves most of their lives, and to accept the new petite bourgeoisie racism, which "makes sense" of the threats to their middle-class respectability as defined by secure and honorable jobs in the educational hierarchy. They are increasingly forced by the pressure of events to redefine their total identity in ways they themselves would have found despicable in the past.

Police, both white and black, are in much the same position. Ostensibly the white policeman is expected to enforce the law without fear or favor, objectively, impersonally, and without regard to race, creed, or economic class. In fact the pressures for discreet leniency to whites especially in the middle and upper classes and permitted severity to blacks favor those groups, classes, and races that control the governmental structure. The problem of discrimination in law enforcement is only a problem to white police officers to the extent that they have internalized the code of the impersonal, nondiscriminatory rule of law. If the white policeman has not internalized that code, he escapes the nut-cracker. In the South, policemen are hired who share the values of segregation and discrimination. Problems have arisen only as they came under the spotlight of northern publicity and local protest. They were forced to preserve the appearances of legality, a demand with which relatively few white southern policemen have been able to comply. In the North, the increased number, articulateness, and political power of blacks have forced white policemen to reckon with the demands for equality before the law.

White policemen, individually and through their professional organizations, have resisted such demands. The use of public demonstrations, publicity, and civilian review boards constitute, it is argued, a limitation on the effectiveness of police in maintaining law and order and in preventing violence in the streets. This publicity and these procedures invite suspensions, arrest, and dismissal of white policemen when they are "only doing their duty." In the meantime, young black hotheads and disenchanted white radicals and Yippies provoke cops to actions that go beyond the code of proper police behavior. The courts, acting under guidelines provided by recent decisions of the Supreme Court, raise standards of evidence and police procedure that limit "police freedom" in making arrests and securing convictions. Newspapers, "bleeding heart" liberals, and white politicians who cater to the opinion of the blacks all hem in the police in the execution of their duty.

But in addition to all of the above, the cop is a human being— in all the connotations of that term. Police work, as Nicholas Alex reports here, is a relatively low-prestige occupation. It attracts personnel to whom the income, security, and prestige is, however, greater than they might otherwise achieve. Police work has historically attracted white immigrants and their children, who used police work as the first step in the process of achieving mobility in American society. As salaries have risen, and as these groups have moved into the upper levels of the police hierarchy, white policemen have begun to achieve a stake in society. As immigrants and, now, as the children of immigrants, they see new groups coming to the fore in urban society. They see these new groups—blacks and middle-class radical students—as less "American" than they, as having little respect for the proprieties of lower middle-class life, for the law as they define it, and for the policemen themselves as whites and guardians of the law. Blacks are increasingly competing for living space in the metropolis and the black ghetto is increasingly expanding as migration from the South and as the high birth rate among the blacks continue. Thus the white policeman flees the expanding ghetto that is spilling into the living space of himself and of the ethnic community into which he was born. In the meantime, blacks provoke him, demand equal protection of the law and denounce and abuse him when that protection is forthcoming.

It is no wonder that the "all too human" white policemen are all too often anti-black, brutal, and provocative, and that they share increasingly in the racist attitudes of the new petite bourgeoisie. It is no wonder also that they resent the "invasion" into their ranks of black policemen who, in following a police career, both weaken the prestige of the occupation and threaten their virtual monopoly over it.

But it is black policemen, the blacks in blue, who experience the nut-cracker of contemporary history in its deepest and most pervasive sense. The very conditions of discrimination, segregation, and lack of opportunity make police work attractive to them. As this study vividly demonstrates, it is the lack of alternative opportunities and the only recent possibility of gaining employment at relatively secure and well-paying civil-service jobs that makes police work attractive at all. Black policemen were motivated to enter police work more by the lack of alternative opportunities and by the relative absence of discrimination in civil-service employment than by any positive characteristics to be found in police work itself. They were aware that, all too often, blacks have felt that the police were agents of a repressive white society. They were also aware that pressures to employ black policemen were in part caused by the difficulties in recruiting white policemen and by political pressures on the department to appease black voters by making a number of civil-service jobs open to them. They were also aware that a job in the department was designed to help control the black community, to deal with black criminals, and to take the pressure off white cops in dealing with blacks. As a result, they entered their jobs with few illusions and little enthusiasm. Once they entered the force, they were in the nut-cracker. Yet they knew at the time that a police job, despite these disadvantages, was the best they could obtain. On a day-to-day basis they were subject to the disrespect and condescension of their white colleagues.

But police work is dangerous work which requires absolute trust and dependability between partners, regardless of race. It is amazing how, as the interviews in this study describe, white and black policemen transcend their differences in dealing with the objective dangers and requirements of police work, how the requirements of work, the occupational role, operate to create a discipline and an occupational character that transcends personal differences, racial antagonisms, and political ideologies. But surrounding the occupational core of the black policeman's roles are a set of cross pressures, role contradictions, and marginalities that threaten his original justification for entering the force. The black policeman sees the force as dominated by a white, primarily Irish, officialdom which places every possible obstacle in the path of his advancement. He is given the worst beats, restricted to foot duty, given little chance to enter specialized services—the Detective Bureau, for example, the Homicide Bureau, or the Safe and Loft Squad. He is most frequently assigned to ghetto communities where he is used to maintain "law and order." All too often, he is thought to be Mr. Charley's boy, the white man's stooge, an agent of the white community, used to oppress and repress his friends and neighbors. There, more than the white cop, he is the object of provocative behavior on the part of black youth. These youth would like to see him lose his control and thereby prove he is the white's stooge, or con him into not making valid arrests on the basis of a presumed racial identity. If he is a "soft touch," he is sneered at because he has been conned. If he is exposed to these situations in the presence of white cops, the white cops will also judge him as "soft" or lacking self-control. At the same time, the white cop allows him to make the arrest, or undertake violent action against another black, in order to avoid racial incidents or charges of police brutality.

In white neighborhoods the black cop finds it hard to gain recognition as a policeman. Too many of his white clientele find it hard to believe he is a policeman. At times they refuse to accept his aid because he is black. At other times, if he is in plainclothes, he risks being shot at as a prowler by white cops who do not recognize him. He is forced to produce his I.D. card in situations where a white policeman would not, and, finally, he is forced to ask his white partner to make the arrest of white offenders because white offenders deny that he can be a cop. As a result, he is forced to share the credit for arrests in white neighborhoods and to bear the risks and humiliation of being considered a traitor in the black ghettoes.

The black policeman, therefore, can never escape his racial identity while serving in his official role. But in the black community, he can never be a simple human being—he is always a cop. Perhaps the most poignant pages in this book are those that describe his off-duty hours. He attempts to escape his uniform as soon as possible after his tour of duty. He avoids the friends of his youth in order to avoid learning of criminal behavior. His friends avoid him for similar reasons, or because they think he is a stooge. He does not socialize with white cops in his after-duty hours. In short, he is drawn into an enclave of black cops, he becomes a member of a minority group within a minority group. Thus, he is doubly marginal. The black policeman does receive some recognition from other middle-class blacks because he has "made it" into the middle-class world, especially in having to work with and in the agencies of the white community. These gratifications, however, are minimal.

The black policeman, as revealed in the interviews presented in this study, is completely aware of the contradictions and incongruities in his position. The inescapable double marginality of the black policeman forces him to become aware of himself and of his social relations. As shown in these interviews, the black policeman is unusually honest with himself, and rarely permits himself the luxury of self-pity or self-deception. Such objectivity does not interfere with his self-identity as a black. He identifies with and, to the extent that is possible, participates in the civil-rights movement. But he limits the extent of his participation to those actions he feels are legal and to those that will not reflect adversely on his occupational role. His double marginality, however, forces him to experience the nut-cracker at the point of severest pressure. As a policeman, he is forced to keep the peace at demonstrations and riots. He may see his friends and family on the other side of the barrier and be forced by his position, by the scrutiny of white cops, and by the provocative behavior that emerges in riots to club and beat those demonstrating for causes with which he essentially agrees.

The picture that Nicholas Alex and his forty-one blacks in blue present to us documents fully and deeply what it means to be placed in a nut-cracker of history. Yet these black policemen appear not to have cracked under its pressure. Apart from their objectivity, they display a kind of gallows humor, an irony that is possible only among marginal men. As far as their work is concerned, most respond to the pressures that operate within it. They try to be objective, detached, and impersonal in their work. They consciously attempt to curb their anger, their sense of outraged pride, and defensiveness in order to avoid becoming victims of their situation. When they temporarily become such victims, they become aware of it. As a result, they seem to transcend those situations that would force them to lose self-control. Some attempt to be human buffers between the world of the police and the world of the ghetto. A few admit that the provocative behavior of black youth enrages them to a point where they may become more punitive than white cops. At these times they become victims of their double marginality. But I have no doubt that as a group they are good cops, New York's finest.

Nicholas Alex, a white sociologist, has done an impressive job of eliciting and analyzing his data. His interviews smack of candor, authenticity, and validity. His analysis is by far the most perceptive study of racial etiquette I have read since Charles S.

Johnson's *Patterns of Racial Segregation* and Ralph Ellison's *The Invisible Man*. But *Black in Blue* deals with race etiquette in a world in which blacks no longer accept a white-imposed race etiquette or a personal invisibility implicit in racial stereotypes. It is unfortunate, but of course necessary, that Dr. Alex has confined his study to the black policeman. The extent and manner in which blacks in other occupations face the nut-cracker of history is not known in the same depth as we now know about the black in blue. At the same time, we know relatively little about how white groups, including the white policemen, face the same historical situations.

Dr. Alex has given this extremely valuable picture of crises in law and order by focusing closely on the policeman. But simply because he focuses so closely on this aspect of the problem, we as readers are likely to lose sight of other aspects of "law and order," including the total picture. This is not intended as a criticism of *Black in Blue*, but only as a caution in interpreting the study. Police law enforcement is only one small part of the entire issue of law and order. Certainly the role of the courts, the D.A.'s office, and the availability of legal aid are other important aspects. Even more important is the content of law itself, and the legislative and political processes that make of the law an instrument of either opportunity or repression. Certainly the availability of the law as a means by which people seek to achieve their legitimate aspirations is a major factor in securing obedience to and upholding of the law. More repressive laws and law enforcement are no substitute for intelligent substantive legislation. The escalation of legalized repression can only result in the escalation of counter-violence, and, ultimately, in a society that has become completely repressive. Some time before that repressive state arrives, the black in blue, regardless of his strength, will be unable to resist the nut-crackers of history.

Joseph Bensman
THE CITY UNIVERSITY OF NEW YORK

CONTENTS

xxiii

BLACK

IN

BLUE

1

The policeman in
the community

This book is concerned with the stresses and strains to which the Negro policeman is subjected as he tries to be a policeman in a society that has not solved the dilemmas arising from contradictions between racial beliefs and democratic values.

First, however, it is important to examine briefly some issues and problems that arise in defining the role of the police in a setting within established societal conflict. What factors contribute to the policeman's role as an instrument of constraint—that is, as an agent sworn to support a given set of institutions; and what causes the community to be suspicious of the policeman and, indeed, of the police function itself?

3

Everyone is aware of the necessity of law enforcement and the role of the law enforcement worker in creating and maintaining social order. The police are aware of this important role of social control for the considerations of general welfare and social survival. Their own educational literature, propaganda, and public relations devices emphasize that they protect life and property, preserve peace, prevent crime, detect and arrest violators of laws, enforce laws and ordinances, and safeguard the rights of all individuals.[1]

However, the abstractions general welfare and social survival have specific meanings in social structures in which there is, in fact, an unequal distribution of wealth, privilege, and power. In practice the police function helps maintain this structure.

This perspective emphasizes the view that the role of the police may best be understood in terms of the community in which the designated police services are fulfilled, and in which police agencies are a part. Hence one should look at the dominant value system in the community and the structure of authority that controls the police, but which the police help to maintain. On this basis the following two questions will be considered: What is the structure of law and order from the point of view of the dominant groups that demand and depend on this service; and what is the relationship of the police to those groups that employ this service as well as to those other groups who do not occupy dominant positions?

Essentially, the dominant groups in the community want and need order and stability in society. The need for order and stability reflects their social positions[2]—that is, those who possess advantages wish to protect these advantages.

Laws, as a specific class of norms, serve to uphold the existing social order by which these groups derive benefits. By nature these

---

[1] J. Edgar Hoover, *Should You Go into Law Enforcement?* (New York, New York Life Insurance Company, 1961), p. 5.

[2] Karl Mannheim, *Ideology and Utopia* (Harvest Books: New York, Harcourt, Brace & World, 1936), pp. 29, 196-197, 205-208.

norms are conservative[3]—they place a high value on the maintenance of stable social patterns.

The law serves not only to maintain this quality of order, but the law in itself legitimates a perspective. In other words, it doesn't matter whether the law is right or wrong, but once a form of behavior is enacted into law by groups that have interests in that behavior, its existence as law gives it a halo of morality.[4]

Less favored groups will tend to perceive the law as repressive, especially in situations of conflict, and where conflict becomes intense the police will be defined by dominant groups as agents who will control those perceived threats to the existent structure.

The policeman operates at the lowest level of law enforcement to maintain a specific structure of order and also to impose the prevailing perspective of law and order on recalcitrants. In short, the dominant groups, by their greater power, have at their disposal public agents who enforce previously enacted legalized social policies by legally prescribed means.

THE POLICEMAN AS A BUFFER

The policeman embodies and personifies "the law." Either in or out of uniform he is, quite simply, empowered to enforce the law. He is a symbol of authority to the extent that he has the right to use a gun when necessary. He is more than a symbol, he is an agent, for he embodies the sovereign right of the state to take lives.[5]

Thus the policeman's official reason for existence is to carry out the law as it embodies those policies and interests which the

[3] James Coleman, "Community Disorganization," in Robert K. Merton and Robert A. Nisbet, eds., *Contemporary Social Problems* (New York, Harcourt, Brace & World, 1961), pp. 592-593.

[4] A. V. Dicey, *Lectures on the Relation Between Law and Public Opinion in England During the Nineteenth Century* (London, Macmillan, 1948), p. 44.

[5] Max Weber, *From Max Weber: Essays in Sociology,* trans. and edited by H. H. Gerth and C. Wright Mills (Galaxy Books: New York, Oxford, 1958), pp. 77-82.

dominant groups wish to protect. This also means that when laws are broken, the people who are protected by the law do not have to deal directly with people who break the law, but need only call in the legitimate representatives of the legal order. While the dominant groups are being protected, they can hold themselves aloof from the actual police work necessary to enforce the law. This implies that the policeman essentially operates as a buffer to protect the dominant groups in the community from potentially disruptive elements that may threaten or harm the quality of order, stability, and peace these groups require. They are also isolated and protected from exposure to obscene, brutal, and violent situations involved in law enforcement. Let us look at this more directly.

The middle and upper classes separate themselves from the lower classes and minority groups, including the Negro, by residential segregation. However, they use the metropolitan community, especially its downtown or midtown area, as a site for business operations and as a source of real estate values. Hence the dominant groups want order, stability, peace, and a continuance of routine operations.

The lower classes, especially new immigrant groups, are, at times, a threat to that order. When members of these groups engage in crime, they do so in ways that reflect the specific patterns of their peasant backgrounds.[6] This, coupled with the fact that they have been confused and upset by their experience of migration and urbanization, results in the type of disorganization that is defined by the middle and upper classes as criminal behavior. Lower-class crimes have tended to be crimes against persons involving violence and petty crimes against property.[7] However,

[6] Gaetano Mosca, *The Ruling Class*, trans. by Hannah D. Kahn, ed. and revised by Arthur Livingston (New York, McGraw-Hill, 1939), pp. 11-13. Also see Oscar Handlin, *The Uprooted* (New York, Grosset & Dunlap, 1951).

[7] For a survey of facts and theories regarding the relationship of crime to race and nativity, see Edwin H. Sutherland, *Principles of Criminology*, revised by Donald R. Cressey (Chicago, Lippincott, 1960), Chap. 8. For a study comparing the rate and type of crime committed by first and second generation immigrants, see E. H. Stofflet, "The European Immigrant and His Children," *The Annals of the American Academy of Political and Social Science*, Vol. CCXVII (September, 1941), pp. 86-87.

when such criminals become more assimilated, their pattern of crime shifts. Crimes become better organized, involve stabilized routines and permanent organizations, and take on a rational economic character. In short, they become organized crime by adopting the characteristic American business pattern.[8]

Middle and upper class crime, in contrast, will be less against persons and more against property. It will be "legal" and abstract, and will often involve the advice of lawyers or accountants, and is called "white-collar crime." It includes stock market manipulating, tax evasion, swindling, fraud, forgery, and evasion of administrative rulings of such government departments as The Federal Trade Commission, The Federal Communications Commission, and The Food and Drug Administration. It is normally not considered by the middle classes to be criminal behavior. The white-collar criminal may be educated, speak excellent English, have a high position in the community, be civic-minded, and may only be thought of as a criminal by members of the lower social classes.

The Negro in the urban area, because of the recent nature of his migration to the North, is almost always found in lower-class positions. His rural background, and the confusion engendered by the new standards of the city, are typical of the reactions of the "peasant." His problem, however, is intensified by his long history of exploitation, segregation, discrimination, and denial of opportunity.

Exposed to the visibly better standards of life in the city, he becomes more aware of the misery of his position. Thus, suppressed resentment is likely to flourish. The Negro adopts the classical patterns of "peasant" criminality, but his resentment also erupts into "race riots." These riots, more often than not, are senseless collective acts of resentment, with little political purpose, being for the most part forms of self-expression usually triggered by overcrowding, "long, hot summers," lack of routine activities to occupy the time, density of crowds in the streets, and

---

[8] For a discussion of white-collar criminality, see Edwin H. Sutherland, "Crime and Corporate Organization," in Robert K. Merton and others, eds., *Reader in Bureaucracy* (Glencoe, Ill., Free Press, 1952), pp. 419-422.

occasionally a specific incident which involves the aggressions of a white or group of whites against a "defenseless" Negro.

All this occurs while the middle classes attempt to isolate themselves from settings in which they would be exposed to the kinds of crime that are most prevalent among the Negro "peasant" groups.

By virtue of their residential propinquity to the urban ghetto, the earlier immigrants who are members of the working class or lower middle class are not able to isolate themselves from the presence of the Negro. They feel the threat at more intense psychological and social levels, in part because their physical and psychological isolation from the Negro is less than that of the physically distant middle classes, and because they are not too much or too long removed from the economic class level of the Negro. Together with the white middle classes they put pressure directly through the political apparatus on the police to keep themselves isolated from "lawlessness," in the particular form they identify with the Negro.

The police then serve as a buffer. Their job is not only to inhibit and minimize crime, but also in part to contain crime within an area where it is less likely to be a threat to the person or property of the dominant groups in the society.

THE POLICE AS AN OCCUPATION

The formal code of police ethics demands complete impartiality and objectivity in the field, but the policeman sees himself as being in a dangerous situation and has to protect himself with whatever means are available.

Because his work requires him to be preoccupied with actual and potential violence he may find himself employing unnecessary force in making an arrest. Such "vigorous" law enforcement may be seen as justified by the policeman on the basis of the department's "relentless prosecution of criminals." The department is usually sensitive to the press and other mass media which it may

8

view as an indicator of the desires of the community. If newspaper reports tend to be critical of the department for failing to
make arrests and stop "major" crimes, then the whole department is directed toward eradicating the cause of the accusation
or proving it to have been misapplied. This places direct pressure
on the policeman to "produce"—that is, to make arrests—often by
disregarding the civil liberties of his "clientele."[9]

Violence is often used on those who are less powerful and
privileged. Middle-class persons are more likely to evoke police
restraint than the lower-class, including Negroes. More often than
not, this is the result of the policeman's appreciation of class differences. He may become "partial to some categories of people
more than others." Those who "get the breaks" even if they have
to be arrested, may be well-dressed, educated persons of higher
social and economic status.[10] This is not to deny the fact that in
given circumstances there are many instances of individual acts
of kindness to lower-class persons—the key is the difference between the police as a group and the idiosyncratic behavior of individual policemen.

The policeman must also be seen in another perspective as
generally having been recruited from immigrant groups for
whom joining the police force is one of the first steps toward
acquiring higher status in a world where they have little opportunity for entree to business or the professions. So in American
society the "policeman's lot" is reserved for the second generation
American, and often third generation. Thus the stereotype of
the "Irish cop."

Part of the pride of the policeman in his occupation derives

[9] Jerome H. Skolnick, *Justice Without Trial* (New York, Wiley, 1966),
pp. 164-181, 237.
[10] For data supporting these assertions, see Joseph H. Fichter, *Police
Handling of Arrestees* (New Orleans, Loyola University of the South, Department of Sociology, March, 1964). Skolnick, *op. cit.*, pp. 80-86 offers
a discussion of the racial bias of white police officers toward the Negro. For
a general discussion of why police use illegal violence, see William A. Westley,
"Violence and the Police," *The American Journal of Sociology*, Vol. LIX
(July, 1953), pp. 34-41.

from the mobility it offers. It is also derived from the prestige associated with the public image of the policeman as a guardian of society. Thus his occupational role compensates for the disadvantages of his ethnic position.

The position of the second generation policeman is reinforced by the fact that at the level of the beat, where he must deal with violent personal crimes and petty crimes against property, he interacts with a class or ethnic group whose arrival to the urban scene is later than his own. Thus the striving for mobility of the lower group is a threat to the newly arrived group to which he belongs. He has a special reason to focus his anxieties and aggressions on the lower group since they do in fact commit most of these criminal offenses which he deals with on the beat. The lower group is therefore his "natural" enemy. In addition he sees them in terms of his own needs for status affirmation which they threaten. As a result, he may develop the psychology of the "redneck," and use his power—the right to bear arms and to inflict violence legitimately—as a major means of personal affirmation.

THE POLICEMAN'S JOB IS UNCERTAIN

Policemen often feel there is a considerable amount of ambivalence or suspicion on the part of the community about them and their function. On the one hand, they have been praised by an "appreciative public" for doing a good job in keeping order. On the other hand, they frequently feel that their sphere of operations and psychological position as guardians of the social order have been threatened by attempts to limit police power, and by protests against police brutality. This "inconsistency" has been frequently noted by the police (individually and through their organizations) who have described the policeman's role as essentially in the center of "opposing social forces." To quote a few of these comments in full:

> I'm sick and tired of giving in to minority groups with their whims and their gripes and shouting. I don't think we need a

10

civilian review board at all. Any civilian review board that has civilians on it is detrimental to the operations of the police department.[11]

We mollycoddle young criminals and release unreformed hoodlums to prey anew on society. The bleeding hearts, particularly among the judiciary, are so concerned for young criminals that they become indifferent to the rights of law-abiding citizens.[12]

I'm only a cop, but you look at me real close and you will see something that has more power than even the President of the United States. I have the power of life and death. In ten seconds, I can kill someone or let him live, and I don't have a jury or a judge or anybody there to say yes or no. You give me this awesome responsibility but you don't want to pay to hire the very best. You cry police brutality without knowing what is happening. You talk about crime in the streets but you tolerate courts giving criminals a slap on the wrist. You don't know what a cop is for or what he should do.[13]

The above quotations convey to a degree the fact that the policeman feels his own lot is not a happy one. While these issues are not logically inconsistent, they tend to evoke conflicting feelings among policemen who must somehow learn to reconcile and accommodate themselves to them.

Objectively speaking, the policeman's perspective may be a valid one. Indeed, there is considerable ambivalence on the part of the community about the policeman and his function; in a democratic society people are leery of armed groups, whether army or police forces. How much autonomy does one grant an armed group—a group which by virtue of its function must be armed?

In order for the police force to function effectively, it requires, by virtue of its professional inclinations and standards, a certain

[11] A statement made by the President of the Patrolmen's Benevolent Association as reported in *The New York Times*, May 9, 1966.
[12] A statement made by J. Edgar Hoover as reported in *The New York Times*, September 5, 1965.
[13] A statement made by a New York City policeman as reported in *The New York Times*, September 5, 1965.

degree of autonomy. Civilian review boards, as well as other forms of restraint, are considered a form of "interference,"—even the interference of their political superiors, the democratically elected officials of their society. Yet by the very nature of police function and the power of the police in relation to different groups in the community, it becomes necessary to regulate and control them—in effect, to "police" them.

The autonomy that the policeman has at the neighborhood and block level often allows him to lapse into illegitimate uses of his power.[14] Consequently there arise problems of the relations of the policemen to various groups in the community, the degree to which he accepts their demands and provides them with a service or conversely, the extent to which he uses unnecessary force or even "brutality" against them. While whites are often suspicious of him, Negroes are more suspicious. The desire among Negroes and Puerto Ricans for the formation of an independent civilian review board is a strong indication of this suspicion. The proponents of such a board have concluded that it is necessary in New York to protect them from alleged "racial insults" and "police brutality."[15]

Thus there is, on the one hand, an element of suspicion on the part of the community toward the police as a "tool." On the other, they recognize them as an independent body of professional practitioners who have the right to bear arms, to inflict violence legitimately, and to operate in terms of their own departmental rules and regulations.

This ambivalence or suspicion of the police by the public contributes to the marginal nature of the job. But there are more easily seen factors that make the job marginal. The fact that the police are not given prestige in accordance with the importance

[14] Joseph Goldstein, "Police Discretion Not to Invoke the Criminal Process: Low Visibility Decisions in the Administration of the Law," *The Yale Law Journal*, Vol. LXIX (1960), pp. 543-594. For a comprehensive bibliography on police discretion, see Donald J. Newman, "Sociologists and the Administration of Criminal Justice," in Arthur Shostak, ed., *Sociology in Action* (Homewood, Ill., Dorsey Press, Inc., 1966), p. 180.

[15] Walter Gellhorn, "Police Review Boards: Hoax or Hope?" *Columbia University Forum*, Vol. IX (Summer, 1966), pp. 5-10.

of their function is a reflection of this ambivalence. Indeed, this was pointed out by the North-Hatt-National Opinion Research Center study of a cross section of Americans who were asked to ascertain the prestige rankings of ninety occupations. The study indicated that the policeman was ranked fifty-fifth on the order of prestige, or a little above the plumber and not too far above the garage mechanic.[16]

The reasons for low prestige, however, are different for different groups. First, it is probably true that the policeman is criticized by members of his own ethnic group, and more generally the recent arrivals, for not providing sufficient order and protection from "crime" as they associate it with the Negro. Therefore, some of the criticism may come from individuals of the lower and lower middle classes. Second, when one considers police work as an initial stage of entry into channels of upward social mobility, the policeman performs necessary but undesirable functions. And since its own patterns of mobility have passed the level of the policeman either because of education, access to business operations or capital, the more established groups look down at the policeman. Third, lower-class Negroes may be critical of the police role because of what it represents, in the sense that the policeman is viewed as protecting the interests of dominant groups in the community, and "either ignores or opposes" the interests of Negroes.

It is now possible to confine our discussion to the nature of the role of the Negro policeman. His marginality is much more pronounced; therefore he presents a crucial case in the marginality of the police.

THE NEGRO POLICEMAN

The Negro who enters into the police role is subject to all the tensions and conflicts that arise from police work. Moreover, the conflict is compounded for the Negro: he is much more than a

[16] Paul K. Hatt and C. C. North, "Prestige Ratings of Occupations," *Man, Work and Society*, in Sigmund Noscow and William H. Form, eds. (New York, Basic Books, 1962), pp. 277-283.

13

Negro to his ethnic group because he represents the guardian of white society, yet he is not quite a policeman to his working companions because he is stereotyped as a member of an "inferior" racial category. He may find it necessary to defend his serving as a police officer and to explain it largely on the basis of economic necessity—that this was one of the best paying jobs that was available to him. But often he feels that he is subject to criticism by his ethnic peers derived from premises inapplicable to his situation—that is, they may consider him a traitor to his race because his race does not benefit from the protection that he offers. Yet he may defend his race because he is a Negro and inextricably bound up in the current struggle for civil rights and the demands of Negroes for social and legal equality. It is difficult for him to play both roles. To be a Negro and a policeman is to be subject to double marginalty, and gives rise to some special problems.

Civil service as a mode of mobility

Civil service is an institutionalized avenue for Negroes as it was earlier for whites to move from lower-class positions to middle-class occupational roles into better paying jobs, both at the Federal and local level. Negroes entering into the job market generally choose the *class* of job (that is, the general level of work), rather than the particular line or occupation, and this mobility might apply equally well to Negro firemen, Negro social workers, and Negro teachers at different levels.[17]

As indicated previously, the police job in society at large is a relatively low prestige job. But the *average* prestige of an occupation may be misleading, for the prestige of the job varies with the particular group and is a function of the social position of the rater.[18] For a Negro, a relatively low-average prestige job may rank high, because of his limited opportunities.

Thus the civil service properties of the police job and the low

[17] Nathan Glazer and Daniel P. Moynihan, *Beyond the Melting Pot* (Cambridge, Mass., M.I.T. and Harvard, 1963), pp. 29-44.
[18] Thomas E. Lasswell, *Class and Stratum* (New York, Houghton Mifflin, 1965), pp. 69-73.

14

status position of the Negro may both be important considerations in the recruitment of Negroes to police roles. Hence police work could be considered as an opportunity for the Negro in terms of a relatively high and secure income, financial independence for himself and his family, and an opportunity to pursue an education, or to attain a higher level of education.

Moreover, police work has offered an element of "safety" to the Negro; it has offered him relatively more protection against the hazards of discrimination than jobs in the private sector. For instance, individuals enter the police department via competitive examination, and it is by such civil service examinations that they are able to advance from patrolman to sergeant, then to lieutenant, then to captain.

The egalitarian ideals of the society may therefore be reinforced by the civil service or bureaucratic nature of the office. In the civil service the individual is evaluated, at least formally, on the basis of objective, impersonal norms. He is treated in terms of the uniform application of general principles and laws, and evaluated in terms of his performance. It is how well the role of a policeman is performed, measured "objectively," that counts, rather than who you are as a person.[19]

From the point of view of the Negro, universalism and performance are desired norms. Objectivity, without reference to race, is highly valued. It may reaffirm the Negroes' belief in the ideology of opportunity, give him hope, the desire to strive for higher status, and the opportunity to legitimate himself as a man who can do a job. In sum, it negates in principle the fact of prejudice and discrimination. Whether these formal guarantees of equality of treatment in bureaucratic civil service employment are, in fact, followed, is a subject of considerable skepticism among Negro policemen.

In addition, recruitment into police roles takes into consideration the following social pressures:

First, the demands of the Negro community for more municipal jobs for their members—specifically the desire from segments of

[19] Weber, *op. cit.*, pp. 196-204.

that community to have more Negroes in the police department. The underlying rationale for such demands is twofold: (1) the feeling that the general quality of police work would be increased in Negro neighborhoods without the handicap of racial prejudice, and (2) it affords the Negro community the opportunity to prove that Negroes are capable of sharing in the responsibility for governing themselves.

Second, the need of police administrators to recruit Negroes into the department because: (1) it is an element of good police strategy, (2) it is a realistic adjustment to the demands of the Negro people, and (3) it may allow the department a way of countering threats to police legitimacy by incorporating and promoting Negroes into positions of established authority.

The policeman as the guardian of society

However, the conditions of a good income and the opportunity to pursue an education at the present time must be seen in the context of being a guardian of society, controlled by whites, and used as a vehicle of pressure on the Negro population.

The nature of the police role and its relationship to public authority have already been examined at length. The services that he fulfills as the guardian of established society, and the reason for his existence can thus be summarized as follows: The police officer has a duty, by virtue of his office, to enforce an established normative structure and to maintain that structure and established legal policies through the use of legitimate force on disruptive elements that challenge, threaten, or ignore it. The law is the first line of defense to threats to the prevailing social system and the interests that support it. The policeman operates as a buffer between supporters of the established order and those who threaten it. In exchange, the policeman gets this job, and the perquisites that go with it.

As an extension of public authority, and as an agent of the law, it can truly be said that the policeman is controlled by the law. This means that the Negro policeman, as the official representa-

16

tive of the dominant groups, is controlled by those dominant groups in the community who control the government which he is obligated to serve. Conversely, it means that, because of his job, he may now be alienated or isolated from his own community—friends, relatives, acquaintances—to some extent, and thus the Negro community relinquishes some of the social control over him that it had previously exercised. In this sense, his function would probably be understood by some Negroes as enforcing the status quo, legitimating white authority, and generally doing the "dirty work" of white society in imposing a white upper class reality on minority groups, a reality in which these groups feel they have no stake. So the Negro policeman is viewed as a "traitor" to his race because his race does not benefit from the protection he offers.

At the same time he is a symbol of accomplishment to segments of the Negro community. There is some kind of prestige that Negro policemen receive from their own background. While this may be considered "ambivalent" prestige, not all Negro policemen are considered "traitors" or "finks." Their family may impute prestige to them, and certainly the possibility exists that some middle-class Negroes do so.

It also appears that the Negro policeman is controlled—in the sense that he may perceive that he is being discriminated against on the basis of race in the areas of assignments—by whites *within* the structure and operations of the department. His superiors in the police department may not be concerned with having Negroes occupy jurisdiction over whites but over Negroes, and this jurisdiction over Negroes is supervised by white policemen. The use of Negro-white patrol teams may be not only an element of this jurisdiction, but also the expression of the department's distrust of Negro policemen by the department itself.

In addition, the whole administrative set-up of the police department could be viewed as an attempt to have Negro policemen predominantly servicing the Negro population. It seems however that the higher up the Negro rises in the police bureaucracy, the less chance he has of having jurisdiction over Negroes. One could

17

posit that there may be no direct interest in having Negroes achieve top positions except in isolated cases, where it is politically expedient to demonstrate the symbolic importance of Negro superior officers to placate a dissident and vocal minority group.

The use of the Negro as a means of controlling the Negro population at the level of patrolman could mean that he actively participates in controlling and containing other Negroes through force. It may be that from the point of view of the police department it is better to see Negro officers actively containing other Negroes than white policemen doing the job. The police department has been increasingly concerned with its image. Having white officers "brutalizing" Negroes makes for unfavorable publicity, intensified racial conflict, and more severe problems for the police, their political superiors, and the dominant groups in the society.

Although the container-controller role is essential to the role of the police officer as we have defined it, the Negro policeman may fulfill other functions by virtue of his identity as a Negro. The following observations are offered on how his race may be used as a police "tool."

First, he makes use of his "protective coloration" to disarm Negro violators from declaring that they have been discriminated against on the basis of race. Second, in plainclothes the Negro policeman can be sent into Negro areas. In this way he may have access to information not easily accessible to white officers. It may also be expedient to use him in white areas where his race could allow him to make observations as a policeman without having a police identity: whites do not expect a Negro to be an undercover policeman because of their stereotyped view of the Negro. Third, he is able to keep tabs on subversive groups or potentially violent groups that threaten the existing social structure and to be used as a major witness for the prosecution against the Negro leaders of such movements.[20]

These patterns of expected behavior reflect the structural position of the Negro policeman (that is, as guardian of white society,

[20] Regarding this latter function, I have in mind the well-publicized Black Liberation Movement with Bill Epton as its leader.

and as a controller of the Negro population). In some ways these latter roles resemble those of the "Kapo." The "Kapo" was the inmate official in Nazi Germany's concentration camps.[21] The "Kapo" role has the following components: (1) he is a member of the inmate population, (2) he acts as an overseer entrusted with command over his ethnic peers, (3) he is an extension of the dominant authority, and executes considerable power, but does not make policy, (4) he is rewarded with privileges and promotions, and (5) in order to keep those privileges, he must continously demonstrate his loyalty to his masters: He is often regarded as a "quisling" by his clientele.

The role of the Negro policeman cannot be explained exclusively in terms of these structurally given demands or expectations. His interpretation of his role will vary according to his personal definitions and identifications; that is, not all policemen will define their essential role in the same fashion. We have arrived at three types of policemen derived from our assumptions on how the role may be perceived.

Type 1. Primary identification with the police role. This is the type of individual who selected the police role because this was what he wanted to be. He has had no difficulty in adjusting to the role because he considers this not only his real life but his definitive life. He outwardly identifies with the role, always sees himself as a policeman first. In order to show that he is a good "cop" he may find it necessary to go out of his way in enforcing the law against Negro violators, especially in the presence of white officers. However, he may see his role as primarily one of instruction: this is the "way up" the mobility ladder, and police work is respectable and pays well. In this way he "fights the white power structure from within."

[21] This is the term used in the literature that most directly corresponds to this role; see Elie A. Cohen, *Human Behavior in the Concentration Camp* (The Universal Library; New York, Grosset & Dunlap, 1953), pp. 199-200. However, while this is not the term used by Negroes, the Negro folk society uses almost identically the same concept in "Uncle Tom" or "White Negro."

19

Type 2. Primary identification as a Negro in the police role. This type of person did not select the role. He perceives his recruitment into the department as having been forced because of lack of job opportunities and discrimination in the market place. He has not adjusted to the role although he considers it an economic fact of life that he cannot take for granted as a Negro. He sees himself as a Negro first and a policeman second. He identifies with the Negro community in its struggle for social and legal equality but not with its deprived life styles. He may attempt to resolve the dilemma of occupying a role he does not like by expressing hostility toward civil service, the police in general, and white policemen in particular. For example, some of his comments might be that if he were white he would not have become a policeman, that civil service is the death of one's ambition, and that cops are basically brutal and ignorant. This type of person develops hate for his official role because that role discredits him in the eyes of the Negro community.

Type 3. The ambivalence in identification. He too did not select the role of policeman. He perceives his recruitment into the department in terms of limited opportunities in other jobs, the police job being the best paying job that was available. He expresses ambivalence regarding his police role and his commitment to his ethnic group. However, he is not at war with the police nor at war with the Negro community, but sees himself as accommodating to the pressures exerted from both sides. He may rationalize his position by saying that he is a bridge linking the Negro community to the police bureaucracy. Thus he develops a political imagination of dual role playing by reducing the dilemma of extremes to one of practical and realistic accommodation.

Conflict between ethnic and occupational role

The Negro policeman occupies a doubly marginal position between the marginal police role and his own marginality as a Negro. His existence is divided into two major social positions, and he cannot take either for granted. Each social situation he confronts potentially tells him something different than he expects. He is a man interchangeable with his surroundings, and he performs both roles under inconsistent expectations.

It is a paradox for the Negro that in becoming a policeman he has improved his *economic* status, yet he may justly feel that he has lost esteem. He now becomes, simply by way of mobility, an open and vulnerable target of hostility, abuse, and derision, accessible to all the contradictory expectations regarding his occupation.

Because he is a *Negro* policeman he may be open to the accusations and social judgments of his ethnic peers of being a "traitor," and "Uncle Tom." He is a man exposed to the shame of his race because his official role and the service he offers is not considered in the best interests of the lower-class Negroes who live in the ghetto. He represents not only law and order, regulation and control, but perhaps more significantly, a social hierarchy to his race. He symbolizes to the Negro his own inequities of power, for he represents the protection of the property rights of whites, protects them from attack and intimidation, and responds in deference to their needs. In sum, he becomes to the Negro the most visible symbol of the disparity between the needs of his race and the way social life is organized.

The above implies that the Negro policeman is isolated from the Negro community. This isolation is perhaps due to: (1) the nature of his occupational role, and to the historical nature of the relationship between the police and rural Negroes who have migrated to the North, and (2) the disparity between integration into the white mainstream for *selected* Negroes while the majority of them have not been integrated. To what extent there is a vicious cycle in the American society which allows the cooptation of Negroes under certain conditions, while at the same time denying the majority of them similar opportunities, can only be conjectured. If this is so, it may be a reason why many lower-class Negroes begin "hating" and "distrusting" this person, resenting his "functional" importance and his self-reported income, while they are becoming increasingly victimized.

To come into an authority role may mean some isolation from

21

his own subculture. Yet his arrival as a policeman, performing services for a white clientele, may prevent him from completely realizing the full sense of this role. He may be considered in the eyes of his white working companions, and in his dealings with the white public, as not adequate to the role simply because of their stereotyped view of Negroes.

The purposes of this book may thus be summarized in the following terms:

First, to explore, describe, and analyze how the Negro policeman perceives, confronts, and resolves a state of stress and conflict that is generated by the occupancy of the Negro status and the police status concurrently.

Second, to investigate potential states of conflict for the Negro policeman, their structural sources, and their consequences in his relationship to his occupational colleagues, to the Negro community, and in his dealings with the white public.

Third, to investigate by virtue of the above, the psychological puzzles in the Negro policeman's attempt to reconcile the qualities and actions expected of him in his role as policeman—his identity as a "cop"—with the qualities of self he feels he has as a member of his ethnic group—his identity as a Negro.

The individual Negro policeman, therefore, confronts conflicts arising from the social structure, from his psychological structure, and from the unique way in which that psychological structure is linked to the external social world.

2

The recruitment of
Negroes for police work.

Hating and mistrusting the police has become a way of life in the ghetto. Much of the racial violence that has erupted over the past few years, including race riots, has stemmed directly from the conviction expressed by many "rioters" that the police department is "brutally" anti-Negro. While this feeling may be ill-founded, the fact of its existence and persistence cannot be ignored. This underlies a major problem for the communities and their city governments: how to restore good will and mutual confidence between the city's significant racial minorities and the police.

23

The recruitment of Negroes into the police department may be a means by which this can be accomplished. If the basis of support for policing in our society must come from all members, it follows that police agencies cannot exclude from their personnel members of those racial groups who do not share the dominant goals of the police institution, or who have different conceptions of law, order, and police services.

It is apparent, therefore, that the recruitment of Negroes for police work is not simply a technical matter of manpower needs and allocation best left to specialists in the department to solve. It is necessarily a political question governed by the needs of city governments to create a wider base of community support for the police with the ultimate purpose of avoiding political difficulties and securing peace. The recruitment of Negroes for police jobs flows legitimately from such concerns.

Whether recruitment campaigns for this manpower source are successful, however, depends on the conditions and motivations which determine the Negro recruit's selection of police work as a career. It may bring significantly higher financial rewards, opportunity for advancement, and economic security that may exceed his previous expectations. Further considerations are: the social standing of the occupation, the nature of the work, the socio-economic level of the individual, and the job opportunities that are available to him. In addition, the recruit must be prepared to meet the risks inherent in police work and the onerous tasks associated with the job.

In this chapter we will review the selective pattern of recruitment that the police presents to Negroes. This will require a consideration of the needs of the police organization for manpower as it operates within the framework of politics, the needs and motivations of potential Negro recruits, and the unique way these needs are linked to the society at large. In this view, the police department will be seen within the larger community in which it operates. Changes in department needs and recruitment policy are related to changes in the population from which potential recruits are found. In short, the larger community assists or hinders Negroes in choosing and assimilating police roles, as well as offering a set of directives and limitations to the police department's recruitment policy.

THE NEED FOR NEGRO POLICEMEN

The pervasiveness of conflict between the police and significant racial groups in modern life gives us a clear warning of the destructive effect this can have upon the functioning of our democratic institutions. The distrust of the police department and the hate campaigns directed against the policeman have frequently brought the community to a near state of war. It is therefore imperative that the city governments take responsibility to undo the highly charged negative image the police have among racial minorities with the purpose of creating a broader base of community support; for in the minds of many Negroes who live in the enclaves of the ghetto, the white cop is associated with white colonialism. James Baldwin describes the policeman and his function in essentially these terms.

> . . . the only way to police a ghetto is to be oppressive. None of the Police Commissioner's men, even with the best will in the world, have any way of understanding the lives led by the people they swagger about in twos and threes controlling. Their very presence is an insult, and it would be, even if they spent their entire day feeding gumdrops to children. They represent the force of the white world, and that world's real intentions are, simply, for that world's criminal profit and ease, to keep the black man corraled up here, in his place. The badge, the gun in the holster, and the swinging club make vivid what will happen should his rebellion become overt. Rare, indeed, is the Harlem citizen, from the most circumspect church member to the most shiftless adolescent, who does not have a long tale to tell of police incompetence, injustice, or brutality. . . .
>
> It is hard, on the other hand, to blame the policeman, blank, good natured, thoughtless, and insuperably innocent,

for being such a perfect representative of the people he serves. He, too, believes in good intentions and is astounded and offended when they are not taken for the deed. He has never, himself, done anything for which to be hated—which of us has? And yet he is facing, daily and nightly, people who would gladly see him dead, and he knows it. There is no way for him not to know it: there are few things under heaven more unnerving than the silent, accumulating contempt and hatred of a people. He moves through Harlem, therefore, like an occupying soldier in a bitterly hostile country; which is precisely what, and where he is, and is the reason he walks in twos and threes.[1]

This is not a singular interpretation. A few scattered observations offer further insight on what some Negroes think of policemen, and how they say it.

> . . . A policeman is an object of contempt. A policeman is a paid and hired murderer. And you never find the policeman guilty of a crime, no matter what violence he commits against a black person. In Detroit, you were shooting "snipers." So you mounted a .50 caliber machine gun on a tank and shot into an apartment and killed a 4-year-old "sniper.". . .
>
> . . . Black people doing ordinary, reasonable, peaceful things in this country are attacked by the police, and the police are praised for it. And you talk about giving the police more money and more power . . .[2]
>
> When the people in a Negro neighborhood hear a police siren, they don't ask who is being helped. They want to know who is being punished.[3]

The city governments have attempted to counter this image and possible threat to police legitimacy through the mechanism of cooptation. This technique, long used by politicians to suppress disorder or to quiet internal discord and open hostility upon the

---

[1] James Baldwin, *Nobody Knows My Name* (New York, Dell, 1962), pp. 61-62.
[2] *The New York Post*, October 24, 1967.
[3] *The New York Post*, February 9, 1965.

functioning of society, is a method by which hostile opposition is brought into the organization to voice its criticism.[4] Its major function is to reduce and resolve conflict by eliminating unnecessary hostility and holding unavoidable unsocial conflict to the minimum or diverting it into constructive or, at least, less harmful channels.[5] The recruitment of Negroes into the police department, including the policy determining structure, is the special form this process takes.

The Police Commissioner of the New York City Police Department was recently reported to have described this process: "We can no longer say we are not prejudiced, that we do not practice segregation. We can't just say this. We must prove this. The department must enter into the community and become part of it. We also have to find ways to reverse the process, *bringing the community into the department. This means hearing its criticism.*"[6]

In other words, the recruitment of Negroes into the department is not simply opening up jobs to all members of the community, but also a political necessity for pacifying the Negro community and winning the support of its members. The hiring of Negroes for police work, and the appointment of Negroes to higher command posts, is one way of achieving these results.

The following observations lend support to this view. For instance, over the past few years recruitment campaigns have been intensively directed at minority youths. Most recently, New York City (financed by a $2.9 million Federal grant), in conjunction with the police department, has begun what has been described as "one of the most unique programs ever undertaken by a law enforcement agency anywhere in the world."[7] The program is designed to recruit 1,000 disadvantaged Negro and Puerto Rican

---

[4] James S. Coleman, *Community Conflict* (Glencoe, Ill., Free Press, 1957), p. 17. For a compact discussion of cooptation see, Philip Selznick "Cooptation: A Mechanism for Organizational Stability," in Robert K. Merton and others, eds., *Reader in Bureaucracy* (Glencoe, Ill., Free Press, 1960), pp. 135-139.

[5] Coleman, *op. cit.*, p. 17.

[6] *The New York Post*, April 7, 1966. Emphasis added.

[7] *The New York Times*, March 24, 1966.

youths (many of them school drop-outs who will get remedial reading to prepare them to pass a high school equivalency examination) for a new police cadet corps. It is intended to *"lessen the odds of race rioting* during the summer and to start a tradition whereby Negroes and Puerto Ricans would become policemen— much as an earlier underprivileged group, the Irish, who flocked to the force in the 19th century."[8]

Further efforts to "bring the community into the department" come from the police department's plans to visit campuses of Negro colleges, advertising in local Negro newspapers, setting up information exhibits in Negro communities, as well as visiting churches and organizations. A "recruitmobile" has been sent into Washington's Negro slums, and a new program has been designed to provide police jobs for returning Negro servicemen.

There have also been appointments of Negroes to higher command posts partly to win support of the Negro community. The first Negro to head a Harlem precinct (later promoted to Inspector in command of police forces in Brooklyn North, which takes in the predominantly Negro Bedford-Stuyvesant area) *"followed the riots in Harlem in 1964."*[9] The second Negro appointed to the rank of Inspector was given a newly created post as Community Relations Coordinator of the Sixth Division, which includes the 28th, 25th, and 32nd precincts in Harlem. When asked whether he thought his race was a factor in the appointment, he was reported to have said: "Candidly, I suppose it was. And that's all right with me. The important thing is I think I can improve the situation here."[10]

The hiring of more Negroes, and appointing them to higher positions, has been backed by civil rights leaders, Negro newspapers, and Negro citizens.

When Negro recruits were hired at the beat level in Harlem, a leading Negro newspaper editorialized: "We believe that from our vantage point of being the community newspaper we can feel and report on the pulse of Harlem better than any other

[8] *Ibid.* Emphasis added.
[9] *The New York Times*, September 1, 1964. Emphasis added.
[10] *The New York Times*, June 19, 1965.

media, and it is a pleasure to be able to say at this time that Harlem is in a state of peaceful calm."[11] A Negro chairman of the African Nationalist Pioneer Movement declared: "The assignment of more Negro patrolmen to the Bedford-Stuyvesant area will go a long way to improve community relations with the police."[12]

There is also agreement among many Negro civil rights leaders that the Negro's relations with the police are better than they have been in a long time. In New York, the difference is attributed to the selection of a Negro policeman as commander of the largest police station in Harlem.[13] One civil rights leader reported: "It [recruiting Negro patrolman] has made a dramatic difference. It's more difficult for the inhabitants of Harlem to look upon the police as their enemy when he's the same color they are."[14]

Hence, there are advantages in hiring Negroes for police work since this may lead to greater mutual understanding between the police and the ghettoes, and perhaps enhance the quality of police work in those areas. This could result in better cooperation from minority groups.

The recruitment of Negroes therefore provides city government the means by which it can transform opposition and dangerous criticism of the police into support and compliance. By incorporating individuals from the "enemy's" camp, that is, by opening up a new set of jobs to Negro candidates, it contributes to the viability of the policeman as the guardian of all members of the community. In these terms, it secures peace by means of ensuring acceptance from a hostile group, and also lends legitimacy, hence security, to the police in relation to these groups.

Incorporating Negroes into the structure of the organization and promoting them to higher positions of authority aids the department in establishing a new aura of respectability. Negroes (if cooptation is successful) should begin to esteem the police, while overt hostility is directed away from the organization. Yet

[11] *Amsterdam News*, September 19, 1964.
[12] *The New York Post*, April 7, 1964.
[13] *The New York Times*, September 27, 1966.
[14] *The New York Times*, November 7, 1964.

this may be overstating the case since the favorable responses to the hiring of Negroes may come from the "black bourgeoisie" and not from lower-class Negro youth who are the most vociferous in attacking the police. The recruiting methods used by the city have so far failed to attract large numbers of Negro youth into the police department.[15] A Negro chief inspector stated that in part, many Negro youth are not selecting police work as a career because they feel that Negro officers are "finks."[16]

The police department, however, may not be interested in having Negroes take on police jobs even though their political leaders find it imperative for them to do so. While the department may not want Negroes, once Negroes enter into the department in large numbers, it *accommodates* itself to use them in special ways. It sends Negro patrolmen to work in Negro areas. It uses Negro undercovermen to collect intelligence in Negro ghettoes. In fact, police departments across the country now use black undercover agents to infiltrate black extremist groups suspected of starting race riots.[17] These agents are assigned to subversive squads which operate out of precinct substations that are located in black communities. Thus the recruitment of Negroes into the department serves two diametrically opposed functions: the coopting of Negroes and their promotion to officer status serves to influence the minority community in favor of the department, while at the same time it ghettoizes the Negro policeman, and accommodates itself to use him to collect intelligence in ghetto areas.

Bringing the community into the department has been supplemented by taking the department to the community. For example, the police in a number of cities have intensified "community relations" programs and "racial dialogues" and have been educating officers on the need to treat all citizens fairly. Atlantic City has taken steps in this direction by the formation of a community relations unit within the police department headed by a Negro officer who feels the problem is one of "opening up

15 *The New York Times*, October 8, 1967.
16 *Ibid.*
17 *The Wall Street Journal*, September 2, 1966.

communications."[18] In Los Angeles, since the riots of 1965 in the Watts area, the police department has established Citizens Advisory Councils in Negro slums to give residents a forum in which to express their grievances on police matters.[19] Similar programs are being offered and articulated in other cities. Thus minority groups are being given an opportunity to unburden themselves through talk—to "get things off their chests" and to feel that the department is really interested in them and their problems. Talk recitals are therefore becoming increasingly important (as conflict increases) in maintaining good will, relieving tense feelings, and projecting the image that the policeman is a friend. Yet for all intents and purposes, these devices simply give another appearance to new forms of cooptation.

THE GROWING IMPETUS FOR HIRING NEGROES

The recruitment of Negroes is not simply a measure taken by urban city governments to pacify Negro communities as outlined above, but it is necessarily a *realistic adjustment* to the growing political power of the Negro community, and to the expansion and contraction of labor markets.

The police department can no longer pick and choose Irish recruits from the reserves of semiskilled and unskilled labor that were prevalent during the days of Tammany Hall, which in its heyday recruited primarily from among the Irish who immigrated to the city, and channeled them into the police and fire departments. This unlimited supply no longer exists.

In part this is due to the fact that to many of those now entering the department, the job represents a lowering, rather than a raising, of their status. This is the result either of the decline of prestige of police work, the increase of Negroes into the department, or of the relatively increased social status of the Irish. It

[18] *The New York Times*, April 10, 1966.
[19] *The Wall Street Journal*, September 2, 1966.

may also be partly due to the decline in the immigration rate to this country.[20] The growing eagerness of the city for Negro recruits is given added significance by the decline of the Irish market. This is not to suggest that they have lost their power. The present Commissioner in New York is of Irish extraction, like the last several Commissioners before him, and roughly half of the force of 27,000 men is of Irish descent.

The police department is also adjusting to the pressures exerted by civil rights groups and Negroes themselves for greater participation in the police organization. This readjustment grows out of the fact that the police department has not reflected the composition of the community. While New York had 1,008,344 Negroes as of 1960, or about thirteen percent of the total population in the five counties, one finds that only five or six percent of New York City policemen are Negro.[21]

The department is now beginning to come to terms with the radical change which has taken place in the geographic distribution of Negroes in our major cities. The ten largest metropolitan areas all showed larger proportions of Negroes in their central cities in 1960 than in 1950.[22] And for the first time, a major city—Washington, D.C.,—became predominantly Negro. What this numerical growth of Negroes means for practical purposes is political power (expressed in votes) to demand and achieve public services and jobs at both Federal and local levels. The hiring of Negroes into the department is in part a reflection of this political power.

The recruitment of Negroes has met with a favorable economic market of supply. Because Negroes have been excluded from many other occupations that are advantageous, the lower-class Negro youth in most cities, who frequently are unable to get jobs, provide a substantial reservoir of potential and "eager" re-

[20] Nathan Glazer and Daniel P. Moynihan, *Beyond the Melting Pot* (Cambridge, Mass., M.I.T. and Harvard, 1963), p. 251.

[21] An estimate by Senator Basil A. Paterson as reported to *The New York Times*, February 22, 1966. The basis upon which this estimate was made is not known.

[22] Noel P. Gist and Sylvia Fleis Fava, *Urban Society* (New York, Crowell, 1964), p. 130.

cruits. These persons are in marginal economic positions; when they do work, it is often at jobs for the unskilled, generally in low-level service trades and occupations paying low wages.[23] From the point of view of the Negroes, the political ends of this cooptation are irrelevant. Their awareness of the ends to which they are "being used" is not an issue. They simply see a job that is available.

The economic pull of the police department for the services of this labor market should be substantial and attractive. As of 1969, the starting salary for a New York City policeman is $8,974 annually with increases to $10,950 at the end of three years. Adding to the attractions of the job are benefits in addition to the salary, which include lifetime security, liberal vacation and sick leave, pension after twenty years, and the opportunity for promotion and college education. Those who are not eligible for the city police can apply to the Cadet Corps and receive a stipend of twenty to seventy dollars a week, depending on family size. They are then given a six-month course to prepare them for the policeman's civil service examination and the benefits outlined.

Another factor gives impetus to the selective recruitment of Negro high school graduates or drop-outs. This is the growing competition from recruiters in private industry, banking, and business for the services of Negro college graduates, and the expansion of professional fields for educated Negroes. While this competition exists at the present time, it does not affect our study of Negro policemen who were recruited approximately ten years ago. Yet for the present recruitment concerns, competition does provide a problem in hiring Negroes who easily meet the police department requirements and are therefore the most attractive candidates for police work. This was acknowledged by a high ranking police official: "We'll have this problem of competing with industry. Negro colleges are being flooded by industry. We'll have to sell ourselves."[24]

A recent report on the number and distribution of Negro professional workers in New York City shows that from 1950 to 1960

[23] Glazer and Moynihan, *op. cit.*, pp. 29-44.
[24] *The New York Times,* July 25, 1966.

the total number of professional, technical, and kindred workers increased from 431,019 to 541,221—a gain of twenty-seven percent. But during the same period the number of Negroes in similar positions rose from 14,113 to 26,910—an increase of ninety-one percent.[25] Thus the department may soon find itself in a bind between its limited success in recruiting lower-class Negro youth, and the increasing depletion of middle-class Negroes who are being coopted at a faster rate by private industry.

Hence, those factors which seem to be decisive in the recruitment of Negroes to the department are those which originate within the political realm of city governments to pacify a minority group, and the demands of the Negro community for more public jobs for their members. This provides the framework for the analysis of the reasons that Negroes themselves offer for choosing police work as a career.

REASONS FOR ENTERING POLICE WORK

Most Negro policemen applied for police work only as one possibility among other similar civil service jobs. In entering the labor market they were not aiming at particular occupations but at a general level of work. That is to say, their goal was not police work as such but the benefits of a civil service job. For those Negroes whose aims are to enter the mainstream of American society and to move up from predominantly lower-class positions, civil service is a crucially important path.

Civil service represents to these persons the attainment of a relatively high, secure income, with no lay-off periods, the opportunity for advancement based on civil service examinations up to the rank of captain, and the opportunity of getting an education or continuing one's education either in police science or in some field outside police administration. The strong regulations in civil service requiring nondiscriminatory job practices were also con-

[25] Hubert J. O'Gorman, *Negro Professionals in New York City, 1950 and 1960* (New York, Hunter College of the City University of New York, Urban Research Center, April, 1965), p. 5. Mimeographed.

sidered a crucial factor as the following comments indicate: ". . . they may discriminate in civil service, but they don't take it out of your salary like they do in private industry"; ". . . you knew that civil service would take you on the basis of your qualifications and that you wouldn't run into any stumbling blocks, discrimination against you because of color." In these terms, civil service is an open and public matter, offering economic mobility, a well-defined career pattern, and developed promotions through one's entire tenure via civil service examination.

In sharp contrast to this approach into civil service, these same individuals were aware of the lack of opportunities for them in other jobs. This lack of opportunity, coupled with the pressure to find employment, reflected itself by their taking the first job offered even if it was not congenial. This is only to say that to gain economic mobility they selected a relatively low prestige job that had little intrinsic meaning for them. Thus police work had no meaning in and of itself, but for the external economic meaning of being a member of a class of jobs. Police work was actually considered an occupational area to avoid because it was thought of as a routine job, menial and onerous, limited in scope for the individual with talent and imagination, and the "butt of everybody's problems."

The two operational forces that we have outlined in our general model above, both in terms of approach to civil service and the avoidance of police work, allow us to differentiate two basic types of work orientation: civil service oriented (representing the majority of Negro policemen interviewed), and police oriented.

Civil service oriented policemen

This group chose civil service mostly because of its economic rewards. The attractions of higher income (short and long run), opportunity for advancement (incremental jumps), and economic security must be seen in the general context of economic depressions and the severe lack of other job opportunities. The following selection of responses gives evidence of this view.

35

It was the depression year. I felt compulsed to be a bread winner. I took every possible civil service examination (and hobnobbing around at various jobs). I tried to cash the three-dollar money order that was to accompany a civil service examination application. I was broke. I can't honestly recall any grandiose dreams of being a big fellow in blue. I had no youth gang life. The policeman was to be feared, and I feared him. So, all I could look forward to is a steady income. (10)[26]

My reason for going in was time. I couldn't take the lay offs. I had a wife and a baby to support. These jobs before I became a cop were nothing jobs—and I mean nothing jobs! The only job I count was the last job I had—the job with Continental Can Company. It was a decent wage and the work was not too hard. The police job is the best job I ever had in terms of much more money, and much more opportunity for advancement—the fact that I could go to work everyday, not to worry about the fact that the job may not be there anymore for me the following day. (7)

You heard many times men say that you never get rich on this job. But you can plan on your income because it's steady. Prior to this job, and the interval between the Veteran's Administration job and the police job, I had nine or ten small jobs. They would lay you off. You went from one job to another. Small jobs and not very steady. (30)

Actually, very candidly, at the time I thought of coming in— it was a means to an end. One reason was salary. The other reason—should I decide to stay in it, it had a twenty year retirement plan. (24)

The subjective meanings attached to civil service by this group are not the products of strong motivations to pursue a career in the civil service, much less a career as policemen. Civil service is perceived as a highly circumscribed avenue, an answer to previous experiences of low pay, lack of job stability, and discrimination in the form of lack of access to skilled jobs, higher wages, and better living conditions.

[26] Numbers in parentheses refer to code numbers assigned to men interviewed.

Three subtypes can be found within the civil service orientation. *Type 1* includes those individuals who tried for any kind of civil service job and took the first one that offered itself. That is, they are explicitly oriented to civil service but not particularly police oriented. The men included in *Type 2* are also civil service oriented but, for reasons which could not be determined, did not apply for other civil service jobs. They see the benefits of their jobs as primarily those of civil service and they also are not police-oriented. *Type 3* includes those who are not oriented to civil service directly or indirectly, and who also did not want to be policemen, but saw nothing better.

However, with all these types a lack of discrimination in civil service was mentioned as a determining factor in the selection of this job. In addition, all of these types operate within the assumption that this is one of the best jobs available to them. The following comment is typical of *Type 1*.

> I took the job because of circumstances being what they were. At the time this police work was certainly not quite what I had in mind at all. I did not as a child plan to be a policeman. The opportunities lacking in other fields of endeavor for the most part were the basic reasons that made me take several civil service examinations. One of these civil service examinations was for the police department, and because of the dire need of police at that time, that agency was the first to call me. (29)

Such a response indicates additional motivational patterns characteristic of the civil service oriented policemen, and in need of further examination: (1) that civil service is a highly circumscribed choice because one perceives lack of job opportunities in other areas, (2) that there is no inclination to take on police work prior to the decision, (3) that this was the first civil service job to come through, consequently no choice was ever really made, and (4) childhood memories and contacts with policemen either did not exist, were not relevant in the decision, or were unfavorable.

Regarding the lack of inclination to become policemen, the following statements, although they demonstrate a coupling of motivational patterns, are suggestive of either a passive or critical attitude toward civil service and police work. Since the civil service oriented have taken a job they consider unattractive but whose alternatives are even worse jobs, it is not surprising that there would be a residue of apathy, dissatisfaction, resentment, and even antipolice sentiment. As the following *Type 2* policemen put it:

> The reasons I became a policeman was simply two things: money and security. I actually didn't want to become a policeman. When I got out of the service, my father was pushing for me to go in. My step-father works for the Transit Authority. He wanted me to go but I was against it . . . I just didn't want to be one of the ones in blue. It wasn't that I was afraid or anything like that. There is really no reasons, I just didn't want to be a policeman . . . the policeman seemed to be the butt of everybody's problems. Whenever something went wrong it was the cop's fault and I didn't want to do it. (7)

> At the time the country was in a slight depression and everybody was thinking what the best was at the time. The Negro was thinking that civil service was the best job for him. This was in the 50's . . . I needed some kind of work and this was it. (28)

> It was predicated on the fact that the job I had at the time I got married didn't pay enough to support my family on. I took the examination for civil service. You would have a pension and whatnot as far as a family was concerned. It would have been more security. When I got out of the service in 1946 I could have taken the examination at that time. But at that time it seemed like permanent guard duty. Of course, your ideas change over time. My ideas about the department changed. I thought of it when I was a little older in terms of security. When I was younger I didn't think of it that way. (12)

Certainly such responses are not the product of a careerist orientation, but a reply to the lack of alternatives.

A *Type* 3 civil servant—with no direct or indirect predisposition for the civil service—made the point that it was "just a job" that was available and was quite passive about the whole matter.

> I never cared for this type of work. I didn't have any real eagerness to join it, not that I disliked the job. It was just a job that was available, that's all. And when they called me for it, I took it. (40)

A stronger position was taken by the following *Type* 3 civil service oriented policemen and can be considered the prototype of antipolice sentiment.

> I never wanted to be a cop and I don't want to be one now! I dislike the job intensely! My mother wanted me to be in school. I don't feel like going. Meanwhile, the Transit Authority needed men and I applied. I got the job and started working for the Board of Transportation. Meanwhile I took the examination for cop. (15)

> I don't like the department! What I dislike about the job is that if you have any creativity you can't express it. The department works against creativity. My brother-in-law talked me into getting this job. He told me about the security and the fact that you could go to school at night. I guess you can say that he twisted my arm. I can't really complain I guess. My hours are good, and as far as supervision, I am like my own boss. (22)

Another *Type* 2 policeman—one of those who did not apply for other civil service jobs—gave the following reasons:

> My friend's father was a cop, and this decided me about going into the department. Also you have to look at security, the twenty-year plan, the fact that it's not hard work per se—and this decided me to go in. I went in with definitely mixed emotions. I didn't look at the money they were offering, but the twenty-year plan was the major factor about the job. As far as the money goes, the cops were actually poorly paid compared to other jobs and industries. (1)

The above reply, in addition to repeating some of the typical reasons given by the civil service oriented policemen, for their choice, alludes to the fact that one can get out after twenty years. That is, civil service is a kind of prison that any minority group is in; not even the best jobs it offers prove satisfactory.

In answer to the question, What do you think of whites who become policemen?, the civil service oriented policemen were given the seemingly pleasing opportunity to express some very strong antipolice, anticivil service attitudes. At the same time they stereotyped whites who become policemen as either fools, failures, misfits, or blackjacks. In addition, their answers to this question displayed their feeling that police work is unattractive, but is the best job available. A typical comment follows:

> Back in the 1920's, prior to 1924, when the quota was open, a number of immigrants coming into this country, particularly the Irish—and lack of education, basic education—there was a necessity to create jobs for these people. As the time went on there was still a necessity to provide some sort of employment for those who were not too qualified elsewhere. Therefore, as far as the other ethnic group is concerned, unless it is a case of liking this type of work, this is the only reason. I can't see why these people [white policemen] would come into the job of this nature when there are so many opportunities elsewhere. (29)

Answers included the following expressions of disaster:

> I think he is a fool! The average white police officer is wasting his time if he has any intelligence. Anybody with initiative and imagination should not join the police department. The whole thing, that is, set-up is limited in scope and limited for the guy with gifts and imagination. It is a semimilitary organization. You fall in or you fall out. (38)

> I have spoken to many white boys about reasons for becoming policemen and if I had the opportunity that they have—all the opportunities they have in terms of jobs—I wouldn't

take this job. I would find this job beneath me. A white cop is a failure as far as I'm concerned. He has no status in the community. He is nothing. (4)

Take the fellow you met this afternoon. Here is a boy with a license to teach and he is a misfit in the police department. He took the job with the department because he couldn't get anything else. That's the reason he took the job. He teaches religion on the side for a fee! Most of my feeling is the same for most of the white guys who come into this job because they are not trained for anything else. They would definitely be misfits in private industry. They come into this kind of job to hide behind the shield of authority. If I had the opportunity that they had, I wouldn't be here. We get some sad brothers in this department. (18)

When one policeman was asked, "If you were white would you become a policeman?" his answer illustrated the lack of alternatives for Negroes.

Absolutely not! I would definitely not become a police officer if I were white. I would only recommend a Negro to become a policeman if he had no other experience or if he just had a high school education, if he had no other trade or school. I think a lot of them [whites] may be afraid to face life—afraid to go out in the business world where you face challenges. (15)

The selection of a civil service job is closely linked with the undermining effects of fear and the crises of unemployment, nonexistent jobs, and the economic and psychological insecurity that these individuals have experienced. The pull of economic rewards that civil service presents, and the lack of opportunities outside of civil service limit his choice. The result is a state of conflict about his work, expressed in statements indicating dissatisfaction, resentment, and hostility directed at the position he now occupies. Not only is criticism directed against police work, as our data indicate, but it is also directed against civil

41

service generally. One policeman presented the case for the civil service orientation quite well when he said:

> I think civil service works against one's ambition. You become complacent. I find this true, not only in the police department, but in other kinds of departments. The Negro civil servant is very complacent. They have assumed that they have achieved something. If you notice that the civil rights movement, with few exceptions—the leaders and their subordinates, including rank and file people who are part of the civil rights movement—are not civil servants. Who are they? They are the man on the street, people who work on the outside. They are people who work in outside industry. Now, although this hurts them at times because of their positions, the Negro civil servant is far removed from this. Not aware of this and far removed. (15)

This man's answer suggests a feeling of self-hate for selecting a job that remains intrinsically unsatisfying for him because he cannot find an alternative. There is an incongruency between the needs of this person to define his own goals, and the needs of the department which expects him to be dependent and subordinate. There results an experience of frustration and failure because he cannot express his ambitions or intelligence. But the dimension of conflict or self-hate seems to be extended to include a realization of the political "emasculation" of civil servants insofar as the police role affords a maximum of formal organizational control over his sociopolitical aspirations. This control has the effect of inhibiting protest or preventing it from finding expression while in the line of official duty. However, this additional dimension of conflict only appears because the civil rights movement seems to have evoked his identity as a Negro. In other words, where the movement makes a claim on the conscience of the Negro who is a policeman, there will be additional stress and strain between his occupational role and the views of Negroes which impress themselves upon him or whose views he has accepted.

The above discussion does not in fact explain why these persons selected police work per se. To answer this question requires that we look at a latent factor, namely, the element of chance. Fourteen of this majority group stated that the police department was the first to call them, after they had taken a number of civil service examinations, and that this is the reason they joined the department. It means that they did not feel there was much hope; they took the first job offered, even when they did not like it (*Type 1*). This is consistent with remarks already given, and is further illustrated by the following remarks made by men falling into the *Type 1* category.

> I looked around for the highest paying nonprofessional civil service job available. I took the test for police, fire, sanitation and correction. I passed all the tests, and the police was the first I was called for. (18)

> One of those civil service examinations was for the police department, and because of the dire need of the police at that time, that agency was the first to call me. (29)

Another policeman stated that he stopped his search and made a decision when he found the alternative to be viable. However, the pressure to make a decision because of nonexistent jobs, his need for money, and the police being the first job (trigger event) to come through, clearly limited his choice.

> It was just a matter of obtaining a maximum amount of security and a minimum amount of time. That is, between the time that I took the examinations (other civil service tests), and the time that I was called by the police department. That is, at the time that I took the examination, I had a wife, a baby, and a car. This was the only avenue open to me. So I had to make a decision in terms of the time that I had and the obligations I had. (34)

When one reviews the job alternatives seriously considered by members of this group before joining the force, one finds that the civil service oriented policeman wishes to be involved in some aspect of professional or semiprofessional work. The areas most generally mentioned were teaching and law. One expressed a de-

43

sire to be a commercial artist, one a salesman, one an optometrist, one a radio and television broadcaster, one an electrical engineer, one a photographer, and one wished to own a business.

This suggests that many of these policemen may feel they are working in a job more limited than their capacities. The fact that they had ambitions for careers outside of the civil service shows either that they did not believe that Negroes had job opportunities, or that they thought they had abilities which would enable them to make other job choices.

The reasons given for not pursuing these professional aspirations were lack of openings, discrimination because of race, length of time needed to prepare for professional roles, and lack of money for support during this period of training. The following remarks illustrate these reasons.

> I wanted to get the dollar. I couldn't wait five more years preparing for a teaching career. I needed money in a bad way. The price of books were ridiculous. I had a wife and family and just couldn't make it go. I needed a job and I got one. (37)

> One reason was economics. I couldn't afford to continue my education. I was fresh out of high school—a starry-eyed baby, discontent. A second reason was the lack of opportunity for me in that field. It was impossible at that time for me. The opportunity for Negroes at this time was closed. (38)

However, a *Type* 3 respondent was not convinced in his own mind that he would get a job outside of civil service.

> Well, I thought of being a salesman. But I guess I figured all along in the back of my mind that I would end up in some civil service job . . . I had passed the examination for the police department and it was a matter of time; and I knew I had this job [police]. (27)

As far as childhood dreams or ambitions, there is no evidence in the interview data to indicate any conscious desire among this

44

group while they were growing up to become policemen. While there is no typical pattern of negative experiences with policemen, a substantial number had had unfavorable contacts. However, this is not surprising when one considers the problems confronting Negro youth who grow up in the ghetto in their relations to the police. While obviously not strong enough to keep these men out of the department, the extent to which negative impressions influenced their antipolice sentiment after the men had become policemen cannot be established, and is only ambiguously expressed. Some of the typical comments on this subject follow.

> Until I had taken a test I can't say I had any contacts that might have influenced me later in my decision. The policeman on the beat—some we held in respect and some we ridiculed, and there were some we had no inkling about one way or another. So, as far as I am concerned, I never thought of being a policeman nor any particular experiences that might be something I could say this was it. (37)

> As a shine boy I had unfavorable experience with policemen. A white policeman broke my shine box and I hated him. On the other hand I got to know another cop who was a real man. Exactly the opposite to this other man. He used to talk with us when we were kids. We even played stick ball with him. He would tell us where the sticks were hidden when other cops would come along who wanted to harass us. He worked with us and knew us. (4)

There is no civil service tradition inherited from immediate family or relatives who were in civil service. In each case a personal relationship could be established as a potential source of influence for going into civil service. Out of forty-one policemen, only four had fathers who were working in some civil service capacity (all four were in the post office). The four fathers were evenly distributed among the two types of civil service orientations (that is, civil service oriented and police oriented). Of mothers who were in civil service, the picture is only slightly changed, with six mothers working in some civil service capac-

45

ity, and again, no significant influence toward either a civil service or police orientation.

Of the thirty-seven policemen who were asked whether anyone had influenced them to become policemen, fourteen reported having been subjected to no influence; eleven reported having a friend who was in the department or whose father was either in the department or some other civil service occupation. However, very few of the eleven would say with any degree of firmness that they were actually influenced to go into the department by a friend, except as a possible triggering event, but then only to "start things moving." The remaining twelve were influenced, but not significantly, by relatives, generally coupled with economic reasons. A few among this group indicated being pressured to stay out of the police department. Again, there was no significant correlation between those oriented toward civil service or toward the police regarding the above distribution.

The only thing that could be said besides the fact that family, relatives, and friends played no decisive influence on policemen to join the force, is that policemen are the first of their generation to establish themselves in civil service.

Police oriented policemen

Out of the forty-one policemen, twelve were police oriented. They chose the police occupation specifically, and not merely because of economic considerations. They joined the police department because they wanted to become policemen, because it offered more prestige than other jobs they had had, and because it offered the potential of satisfying their personal interests in youth, community work, and law. Because they feel police work has brought them status and mobility, they identify with the job and the functional value of police service. The ideology of police service and high ideals of this group as a whole could be stated as follows: "A policeman is a friend, to be called on in any emergency. He represents the law and his powers are derived from the mandate of the people. His contact with people often casts him in the role of psychologist, social worker, parent and brother. He enforces the laws—all the laws—yet he does not punish. He stands as a shield between the law-abiding and the forces of evil."

The following reasons given for joining the department substantiate this view:

> From the time I began police work it always appealed to me . . . the duties I suppose. I suppose it denoted a close sense of work in the community. I found them [policemen] showing concern and denoting bravery. I found them friendly and showing concern, and above all bravery. (31)

> The reasons I moved from Transit to City [police] was because I was always interested in young people—youth. What am I saying by this—I always had a way with young people. I could talk to them where no one else could. The Transit police have no youth organization—strictly involved with crime fighting. (14)

> The respect I had for law and order and policeman responsibility. And a latent interest in juvenile work. I was aware of this work even before I came into the police department. I believed that policemen could do more in juvenile work than some of these agencies. (21)

The prototype of this group illustrates overtones of a "calling" with a strong identification with police work and police ideology. One informant stated:

> On the basis of the peculiar mystique of law enforcement. On the basis of a peculiar appeal to those of us who are benevolently concerned with our fellow man. I thought I could, and I think I've had some effect in this concern of mine . . . I never approached the field with the common glamour which is built up. I didn't see police work as glamorous—a dashing job. There is too much hard work involved —unrewarding work—in the sense of your sincere interest to effect changes—to effect changes in people you are in contact with. (9)

47

However, to what extent these reasons reflect a sense of "mission" and strong identification with policing, rather than a rhetorical device to justify to oneself the choice of an occupation, is difficult to answer and its meaning must remain ambiguous.

In answer to the question, "What do you thing of whites who become policemen?," this group said that if they were white they would still become policemen. It also gave them the opportunity of expressing positive feelings toward the department, and proclaiming a relatively good working relationship with white policemen. Further, their interpretation of the difference of opportunities that exist for whites and Negroes in the market place prior to their joining the department reflects a more tolerant attitude than the civil service oriented group. Take for example the following reply:

> You can be in civil service work and not have as good a job as police. I like my job very much. If I didn't like this job I would find something else to do. (16)

Another policeman seemed to be defensive regarding the relationship between whites and Negroes in the department.

> I have a high regard for them because we are friends. I am friendly with them and their kids. We have some close relationships. That is, a few of them are close to us. We visit each other's places. So, if they do have more opportunities than we do, I would take advantage of them. But the white guy may not want to take advantage of them. (25)

A further interpretation was expressed in this way:

> I feel that many white people who become policemen is due for the same reasons that I did. And although I recognize the fact that the white person may have better opportunities, it is impossible for all white people to become successful. And furthermore, many of them don't have the opportunities to advance in other fields. I don't assume that they take the position to wield power, and I would judge that as I see it. (26)

48

Another policeman asserted that the opportunities and aspirations of the two races are the same.

> I think that the average police officer who has more than a high school education, whether white or black, the opportunities in the main are primarily the same. From the educational standpoint, seemingly the aspirations and hopes run pretty much in the same vein. As far as aspiring for promotions—I think they both find it difficult to make promotional examinations, and are both sorry they didn't go back to school. (31)

It is interesting to note that the question dealing with their opinions of whites who become policeman was used by most of the police oriented informants to reassert their positive feelings about Negroes who become police officers. Pride in being a policeman is a consistent theme among this group. That is to say, because he considers the police opportunity as a personal victory over his circumstances of being a Negro, he has more pride in being a policeman. This could be interpreted, however, as the obverse side of his low status in society; the inability to secure greater things as a Negro allows him to make the most of the little that is his as a policeman. Yet the evidence seems to support the former view; that because he is a Negro he has more pride in being a policeman, and has to be better than a white. For example:

> I have found that the average Negro who is on this job is pretty top notch. Because we are screened so thoroughly we have to have a lot on the ball. I am talking about the average Negro as compared to the average white cop. Or to put in another way, if it was not for the quality of the white cop I would have been eliminated a long time ago. The Negro has to be especially sharp. It's that much tougher for him. So if he makes it after a thorough screening, he has to be one of the best. (2)

> I took the job as a cop because they [police department] wanted to keep me off. I guess you could say that is what influenced me to get on the police department, was their trying to keep me out so hard. I passed the examination with

a high grade and they began to investigate me. That's when they got very picky about little things. I had to explain about the scar on my hand from when I was a kid. Then they asked me, did I have a J.D. card, record of arrests as a juvenile. I told them, no. Then this investigator tells me they have a J.D. card on me from when I was fifteen. It took me four days to remember what he was talking about. When I was fifteen, three of us was in the park shooting arrows at box targets on a tree. This cop comes up and told us to get it out, then he asked us our names. We told him and he let us go. He said, "Don't let me catch you all at it again," and that was that. Then this guy tells me, seven years later, that the cop had written out a J.D. card on us. Now that is the dirtiest thing a guy could do! (8)

It should also be mentioned that no one among the 12 police oriented expressed any indication that the police department was the first agency to come through. The element of chance was not in fact a basis for their decision to become policemen. On the contrary, the decision was made by them, and against terrific odds, as their previous remarks have made clear. This stands strikingly against the civil service oriented policemen who expressed the view that the element of chance was a major factor in their "selection" of police work. It will be recalled that the civil servants did not feel there was much hope of finding other work, hence they took the first job they were offered. In sum, the police oriented selected the job out of pride in being policemen, while the civil servants chose the job because they had no other choice.

When we consider their views of the possibilities of job alternatives which they considered before becoming policemen, this group, on the whole, did not consider any other kind of work. Only two policemen considered work outside of civil service before becoming policemen. One of these expressed interest in becoming a medical doctor; however, this was not expressed convincingly. The other, wanted to go into law, said it was "not [to be] a practicing lawyer, but a lawyer engaged in law enforcement . . . there were no obstacles in not pursuing law. I did pursue law for two years. At that time, I thought it was a burden on me financially and it was a matter of pride not to rely on the hand out of the home." (9) And while a few considered other civil service jobs, all were connected in some way with police work.

> At that time, while I was a bus driver, I considered once of becoming a state trooper. I took the examination. I failed the first examination and didn't bother to take it again. (14)

> I took the examinations for transit and correction officer, but was most interested in the transit cop. (8)

Regarding childhood dreams or ambitions, there is scant evidence to indicate a conscious desire among this group to become policemen, or a reflection of a favorable image of the police officer. Hypothetically, positive pre-police impressions could have acted to reinforce their decision to become policemen. Or conversely, it could mean that the pride one has in being a policeman allows him to seek out, in response to the question, all those qualities that are good in the police image, and to suppress all those qualities that are bad.

> I had interest in the police force as a kid. I was always interested in police work. I had previous good contacts with the police. I had no trouble with them at all. (5)

> In Manhattan where I grew up I had contacts with policemen, and they denoted to me bravery. It wasn't too much what happened to me actually, but what happened to friends or people in general. In regards to their concern and kindness when someone got hurt, they were the first on the scene; the manner in which they gave aid and in their bravery. I saw them responding to certain situations of people getting out of hand and making themselves obnoxious. They had the right know-how and exercise of force to quell the situation from getting out of hand. (31)

However, the majority of police oriented indicated no desire to become policemen, nor did the policemen offer them an attractive role model.

51

REASONS FOR NOT LEAVING POLICE WORK

In order to ascertain what keeps the civil servants in the boundary or conflict situation (arising from the fact that to secure for themselves economic mobility they selected an intrinsically unsatisfying job) I asked the question, "What other work have you seriously considered *since becoming* policemen?" The civil servants, on the whole, had considered no other work, not because they liked the work, but because they could find no alternative that paid as well. A small number within this group in dicated that they had or were seeking some other kind of work, either in civil service or outside of civil service, although most of them mentioned getting out of the department only after putting in twenty years. The police oriented, not surprisingly, were unequivocal in not seeking some other kind of work; all of them were pleased with the work they were doing and were concerned with getting promotions. Some of the comments made by civil servants as to reasons for not leaving the police department follow.

> In a sense, it's almost like living from day to day as far as goals are concerned. I think why a lot of men stay on the job is because of security and money. Sometimes I think I would be better off on a job that didn't have so much security and money. It gives you a lot of security but this security makes me a little lazy about looking for another job, or going to school. Suppose I go to school and become an accountant. When I graduate as an accountant I would be making about $125 at the most. As a detective I make about $165 a week. I would think twice about it before I did something like that. It blocks your ambition though. (11)

> This job makes you complacent. You tend to put things off because of no pressure on you to take advantage. Civil service work makes this of you. You feel no danger involved in your being replaced. You don't have to fight for your survival. You are in the job. You feel snug. I don't think this is good at all. I feel that I could do better if only I put myself to it. (40)

52

As far as the long range goal—if somebody comes up with that offer that is much more money than I am making now, I would take it. I am not a dedicated policeman, that's for sure. If the money is there I will go. (38)

The desire to get out of civil service and to become independent is illustrated by the following comments:

I would like to go into the funeral industry because civil service is the death of ambition. I would like to be the opposite of what a civil service man thinks and is. If I had money I would in nothing flat go into the funeral industry. You have to have drive to get into this. (4)

Electronics. I went to RCA. I took courses. I found it was a rough way to make a dollar. I was taking courses in service and repairs. I was doing this because I was trying like hell to acquire a skill. I worked at this for five years. I worked at night repairing sets—audio systems . . . I still like this kind of work. I feel I will still get involved in it one of these days if I make the right connections. (18)

Actually being a sergeant doesn't interest me. The only thing that interests me is financial interest. My goal in life is to go into real estate and insurance, or law, and being my own boss . . . because the police job doesn't excite me. The police job is just a job. (20)

A few civil servants considered going into the fire department. This answer is typical:

The fire department. Matter of fact, since speaking to you last over the telephone, I've been thinking of going into the fire department. The fire department is not as petty as the police department. Not as petty as far as supervision. The police department they say is a semimilitary organization. In other words they base their activity on the army. You always have inspections. You march out to be inspected. A lot of chicken shit. The R.A. [Regular Army] shit—you know what I mean. (7)

Another civil servant commented on his desire to get into the fire department but then rationalized his reasons for staying in.

> Since being a policeman, as I said, I've thought of going into the fire department. Matter of fact, I was still thinking about it when I was in the precinct and on my first assignment, after leaving the Academy. It was still in my mind. Why? A lot of policemen were leaving the police department because they thought it was better in the fire department. For one reason, you could handle another job. Another reason was because it was less work for the same amount of money. You couldn't handle another job in the police department because you would get fired! You can, but it's very risky. I stayed in the department because I figured that the chances for advancement were much greater after all. (6)

The police oriented, on the other hand, considered no other work and are only interested in getting promoted within the police bureaucracy. The following comments attest to this view:

> No. Not even in my most despondent moments. I am unwilling to give up police work, even though I realize I can do other things as well and be financially rewarded to a much greater extent that the rewards that are offered to me now. . . . Since being in law enforcement I had many, many opportunities, but, I can't give it up . . . in the short run, I would like to be assigned to our department of youth division—in areas of youth investigation, and to be promoted to sergeant is the first step . . . in the long run, to become a power in the police department hierarchy—even to become the power of the police hierarchy. I am going to strive to be the Police Commissioner! When the time comes to reach for it, I will reach! I am not saying I will become this. I will strive for this. (9)

> In the department, I would like to go into the Detective Narcotics Bureau and rise to be a superior officer in the department. (5)

54

The city government's need for Negro policemen is thus accommodated by the Negro's desire for decent jobs. The problems of a law enforcement agency under extreme stress, and the personal strivings of a deprived community, bring about a natural symbiosis—the police department and the unemployed Negro need each other. From the point of view of the Negro policeman, however, entering the department under such circumstances is far from satisfactory. But his initial discomfort about the role he is expected to play is only an initial stage to further problems he will face.

═ 3 ═══════════════

The police image

The police department, like other organizations, is concerned with the problems of providing an identity for its members, assuring their loyalty, controlling their actions, and in general, socializing them into a police culture.[1] While these problems are applicable to every member of the department, the Negro policeman raises special issues.

One can understand the department's concern in its efforts to socialize civilians into policemen when one remembers that the negative definitions of police work are characteristic of both Negro and white policemen. We have suggested in Chapter 2 that

[1] See Max Weber, *From Max Weber: Essays in Sociology*, trans. and edited by H. H. Gerth and C. Wright Mills (Galaxy Books: New York, Oxford, 1958), Chap. 4, "Science as a Vocation." Also Howard S. Becker and others, eds., *Boys in White* (Chicago, The University of Chicago Press, 1961).

civil service oriented policemen, by their negative reasons for choosing police work, are uncomfortable in the role they are expected to play. This discomfort is something that starts at the time of their recruitment. If it is to function effectively, the police department must counteract these negative attitudes by creating a positive image of the policeman.

Also, as stated above, police oriented policemen, who initially identified with the police role and expressed a positive commitment to a police career, do not find themselves necessarily exempt from their mutually contradictory roles as Negroes and law enforcement officers. In addition, for these men another potential conflict inherent in their position may arise from that very identification with the police role which others may refuse to recognize. The fact that a Negro identifies himself with the police role does not necessarily guarantee acceptance of his self-definition by his superiors, peers, or the public at large. One may say parenthetically that in order to compensate for this denial of full acceptance, the police department may find it desirable to offer special rewards of both a monetary and honorific nature in order to sustain the Negro policeman's commitment to the service.

The methods of training and control of policemen, as well as the use of their services by the public, involve the existence of accepted definitions of police roles by both the policeman and the public. These definitions consist of norms, which in their fulfillment require individuals to identify with police work, and to acquire the behavior and modes of feeling associated with being a policeman. This means that recruits who enter the department encounter demands for kinds of behavior, motives, attitudes, and beliefs which are new to them. In short, the recruit learns what it means to be a "cop," as defined by his supervisors and peers, the law, and the articulated opinions of society.

POLICE PROFESSIONALISM

The formal articulation of these role requirements has taken the form of an ideology of service and high ideals. Policemen, as

58

members of a "professional" association, fulfill a service function which is vital and intimately related to the welfare of the community, based on an acquired body of knowledge, the formulation of ethical codes, and his professional training.[2] Thus, while the policeman may be criticized by the public, he can still justify his official role on the basis of his professional know-how in maintaining and restoring social order. Therefore, in the face of this criticism he can properly raise the question, What would you do without cops?

This ideology of service constitutes the basis of an occupational self-image, personal and occupational pride, security, and commitment to the organization. It comes into operation, at the personal level, when the policeman questions the worth of his job, or takes seriously the criticism directed against him. It is then that he looks for answers and support to this body of professional ideology.[3] It also acts to prevent questions on the part of the policeman about the meaning of his work and the "services" he in fact renders. Lastly, it plays some part in the choice of police work as a professional career. It will be recalled, however, that only a minority of Negro policemen responded to the department and police work in terms of its high ideals, noble purposes, and technical skills needed to do the job.

The following excerpts of an address given to members of a graduating class of policemen are instructive regarding the general outline of police ideology as it may appear to the department, and the image of moral superiority this ideology provides to its personnel.

You are an armed man in an unwarring world because of the duties and responsibilities of the Department . . . The De-

[2] For a compact discussion of the essential characteristics of a profession, see Ernest Greenwood, "Attributes of a Profession," in Sigmund Noscow and William H. Form, eds., Man, Work and Society (New York, Basic Books, Inc., 1962), pp. 206-217.

[3] For a discussion of the functions of ideology in terms so described, see Howard S. Becker and James W. Carper, "The Development of Identification with an Occupation," in Richard L. Simpson and Ida Harper Simpson, eds., Social Organization and Behavior: A Reader in General Sociology (New York, Wiley, 1964), pp. 252-259.

partment exists for the purpose of guarding the life, rights, and property of the people of this great city . . . It demands wisdom, patience, humor, integrity, and courage . . . It asks you to subdue a good measure of your own identity in order to protect those who need protection—to help the helpless, care for the lost, and assure those who are in fear. On the other hand, it offers enormous rewards, quite beyond those personal ones brought by the doing of good works. If you see that you have a part in the hard labors of the Department; then you'll see, too, that you have a share in the greatness and nobility of the Department . . .

All of us as private creatures know moments of dissatisfaction with ourselves—moments when pride fails us and we are led to doubt the significance or meaning of our private efforts to lead the moral life, to be good. It will be at such moments that you, as cops, will find strength and reassurance in your participation in the larger moral life of the Department. There can be no doubt about the significance of that life, and when the knowledge of that settles in your minds and hearts then there can be no doubt about your own significance . . .[4]

The police department is presented to its practitioners as morally superior and prior to them. This is consistent with the demands of most bureaucratic organizations which proclaim that the organization is more important than the individuals who make it up, and the legitimate need for the police is the moral imperative behind it.[5] But the price one pays for giving up his name and identity to the department's demands for submission and subordination is not without rewards. The department determines correct police procedures, what is the proper and just thing for the department to do in given circumstances which require police action. This allows the policeman to act with detachment by using his vested power without self-consciousness, or feelings of

[4] As reported in Richard Dougherty's novel, *The Commissioner* (New York, Pocket Books, 1963), pp. 66-68.

[5] William H. Whyte, *The Organization Man* (Anchor Books: Garden City, N.Y., Doubleday, 1957), pp. 6-7.

guilt.[6] For he is acting on behalf of and for the department which has declared itself to be more virtuous and legitimate than its agents. The policeman can therefore point to his function and to his institutional position in making claims to prestige benefits implied in that position, without having to confirm that claim himself. In addition, this identification with the ideals of police work may tend to increase to the degree to which the policeman's legitimacy is called into question in specific stressful situations, such as race riots. Further, a significant feature of these riots is the tendency of local officials and news media to escalate their praise of the police in terms of the language of professional terminology. It goes without saying that the effect of the riots has been to make the police more repressive.

The address also enumerates some of the characteristics and functions of police professionalism. The department as a professional association is typified by a similarity of outlook, a community of interests, where language, skill, and technical background are shared. Policemen, by virtue of their associations, are like-minded people carrying out an important service to the community,[7] supported by a code of ethics,[8] involving, to use Harold Lasswell's phrase, the management of violence as a career. Although it may be an art or a science that is learned, what has not been emphasized in the address is that professionals also want to maximize their prestige and income, and to minimize "interference" from the outside.[9] Because of their professional inclinations and standards, policemen attempt to preserve their occupational autonomy by freeing themselves from external constraints, including those of their political superiors in whom the legitimate power of the police is vested.

Within professional bodies, there can usually be found associations.[10] In the N.Y. Police Department the most comprehensive

[6] Ibid.
[7] A. M. Carr-Saunders and P. A. Wilson, The Professions (New York, Humanities Press, 1964), pp. 306, 471-477.
[8] Ibid., pp. 302, 418-422.
[9] Ibid., pp. 357-358.
[10] Ibid., p. 319.

61

association is known as the Patrolmen's Benevolent Association. It has the qualities of a trade union, acting as a bargaining unit for the protection of its membership, trying to obtain higher wages, improved working conditions, and other economic benefits. It also fosters training, attempts to promulgate a code of ethics among police personnel, and acts as the center of power within the department that sets the general direction of department policy making.

It is not unusual, however, to find a number of associations coexisting within a profession.[11] This is particularly striking in the police department, which has fostered a variety of associations based on racial, religious, and national loyalties; on differences in what may be termed professional outlooks among police personnel; on differences in economic levels based on rank and work assignments; and on antagonisms between "insiders" and "outsiders."[12] In this latter regard, a strong possibility exists that Negroes, including other minorities in the department, feel they are not treated on an equal footing with their professional peers. As such, they have felt that they need their own independent sectional associations—for instance, the Negro Guardians—as defenses against the ideological threats or assaults of other associations.

The potentiality for conflict between Negroes and the department as a whole, like the survival of independent associations and ideologies, indicates some unresolved problems of organization which may exist, particularly in terms of the conflict between the official professional ideology and the one perceived by Negro policemen.

Advocates of professional status

The conception of police work as a professional activity was reflected by thirteen of the forty-one Negro policemen in the study who were asked the question, "Do you consider police work a profession?" Generally, in describing police work in these terms,

[11] *Ibid.*, p. 320.
[12] *Ibid.*

62

the advocates of professionalism expressed themselves in terms of the model of police ideology we have outlined, with some few additions. More specifically, they talked about training, educational requirements, and professional course work as their reasons for the evaluation of the professional status of the department. Others talked about a definition of service to the community. And still others talked about a body of knowledge requiring a prolonged period of time and travel to the Police Academy where the policeman learns his skills and how to practice them effectively.

It should be noted, however, that while patterns of social mobility may account for professional ideologies and the social and psychological characteristics of work orientations, there is no evidence to indicate this is so in our data. That is, there seems to be no significant difference between civil service and police oriented types regarding the claims they make to professional status. Nevertheless, the variety of substantive answers to professionalism stands on its own, and offers some further evidence of the special problems confronting Negro policemen.

The following examples suggest that the official body of norms formulated as police ideology apparently enjoys support, not only from the police oriented, but from a number of individuals whom we classified as civil service oriented.

> . . . there is much that goes into police work from many facets that it would have to be a profession . . . The work itself puts it on a professional level. You always find yourself trying to live up to the job. The need is always there and you are trying to fulfill it. . . . No matter how much you learn about police work there is more. There are many facets that have to be reckoned with on a professional basis. You need the expert. (31)

> You are constantly back and forth to that Police Academy. You have to have considerable knowledge in your relations to people in the community. And when you are on the job it is these things you have to do. You still do everything you can to help people. Take a doctor and his work. He has to have education and time in schools. He goes there for a training period. He is guided by certain rules and ethics that he has to

> obey, and it is not who he can pick and who he can treat, but he has to accept what comes his way. This is similar to the police. The training is important here. You are continually learning on this job and you have to apply what you learn. (33)

Still another policeman talked in terms of "multiple role playing" which requires different professional skills, although he was of the opinion that many men in the department have not attained this level of professional virtuosity. While this policeman identifies with all the positive accouterments of service professions and social amelioration, one might conclude that this is a projection of the police image in direct opposition to what policemen actually do.

> You have to be, in order to be a good policeman, a little doctor, lawyer, guidance counselor, and social worker. The circumstances would arise where you would have to use all of these. Even in the medical profession you get the misfits. I would say that the method they use to choose professionals might be overhauled. It is a trying job. But as long as self-satisfaction is there, I think it is a rewarding job. (23)

A number of these men felt that police work was in the process of becoming a profession. That is to say, that the department is primarily involved in competition between the images of the more traditional policy, and a newer, "professional" police policy, therefore suffering the stresses and strains of an evolutionary process. In the context of this evolution from a marginal occupation to professionalism, those who identify with the latter felt free to make some criticism of individuals who were lagging behind. It may be indicative that those policemen who consider the department to be in the process of change may conceive of themselves as the major innovators and initiators of this process. For example, one policeman stated:

> Years ago this job was characterized by a dumb Irish cop. It is still dominated by the Irish, but the calibre of police officer is

> quite different. Years ago he would approach you if you went past a light and chew you out for doing so. But he was too dumb to give you a summons because he couldn't read the forms nor make them out. Today he approaches you in a more polite way and proceeds to give you a summons. (37)

Another policeman placed this process of becoming a professional in the context of the growing awareness and education of the public.

> Well, the fact that the sensitivity of the average citizen is much higher today . . . In other words, people themselves have grown more intelligent, so the patrolman himself has to be more intelligent . . . So, when the citizen becomes more prominent, you have to show you have something on the ball yourself, or they won't listen to you, nor will they have any respect for you. (17)

Another policeman noted the potential tension that exists between less educated, tradition-oriented policemen, and the professionally minded policeman who is more receptive to new methods of police work and more amenable to change.

> The department is in the process of becoming professionalized. For many years, the rank and file police officer with a minimum of Police Academy training learned his trade on the streets—theoretically, under the supervision of a veteran officer and his superior officers. This was not good because during this period which would extend past World War II, roughly speaking, until approximately 1957-1958, there was no specific incentive for self-improvement, save the matter of studying for promotion through the ranks. In fact, degree people were looked to as eggheads. To bring it right up to date— the present Police Academy training is almost indescribably superior to that of ten, fifteen, twenty years ago. There is a terrific lag to be overcome. There are roughly 26,000 men in the department, and I don't have any specific knowledge of what percentage of the men are taking courses at the Baruch School in areas of Police Science and Personnel Administra-

tion. I feel that logically, it is the younger men in the main who are taking advantage of the educational opportunities before them. Of course, there are a greater number of old-timers who are against this, against new methods of police work. (10)

One policeman, who could be considered as completely identified with the police role, elaborated somewhat on the idea of new methods of police work. Here, there is an identification with the language of police professionalism expressed at such a high degree of abstraction that the actual role of the policeman is totally obscured.

It is definitely in the process of becoming a profession. All of this connotes and denotes a profession. It is becoming a profession, mainly because of the efforts of those who are professionally inclined. That is, through their efforts of codifying the job, the work, the idea, of being a police officer—of one kind or another. They have been successful in instilling the idea of training, the technique of supervision, the idea of personal effectiveness, and developing all of this into a whole structure. (9)

Another policeman remarked that the department is trying to transform itself in the image of the Federal Bureau of Investigation.

The department is becoming professionalized. The department has been criticized by the F.B.I. The police department has used this organization as a mark of comparison—and of course we are open to criticism in terms of our crime statistics —to try and have it come up to the standards of the Federal Bureau. Lots of times the department suppresses certain crime statistics and the F.B.I. refuses to accept this. (13)

One policeman in his image of professionalism de-emphasized upholding the law, and emphasized the understanding of those who break it.

66

Through in-service training and personal study—trying to encourage college level men to come into the job. To have a background in dealing with people and not so much in the sense of the upholding the law, but to have a more elastic interpretation of the law. To understand what motivates people to do certain things. They need men with fertile minds—to encourage men to advance scholastically—to have a broad understanding of people. (13)

In sum, an elastic interpretation of the law, new methods of police work, and the different skills that policemen should be proficient in all add up to a professional ideology of service or social amelioration, which may even override the traditional image of law enforcement. The special aspect of this ideology is to be more understanding of people, more treatment oriented, and less punitive in enforcing the penal code. Thus it demonstrates that the police should serve high ideals and noble purposes by helping the deprived and the needy, rather than simply controlling and containing them at the level of the ghetto beat. However, from the point of view of the policeman, the degree to which his identification with social amelioration merely covers the actual reality of social control is problematical.

Ambivalence toward professional status

Professional images articulated into ideologies of work rarely correspond with actual police behavior. For the most part, the police profession, like other professions, operates in terms of a basic set of distortions, or simple fictions about itself.[13] In contrast to those cited above, most of the policemen are aware of this to varying degrees.

Despite the efforts of the department to promote an ideology and the techniques used for inculcating it in their membership, 18 of the 41 Negro policemen interviewed did not subscribe to it.

[13] Harvey L. Smith, "Contingencies of Professional Differentiation," in Sigmund Noscow and William H. Form, *op. cit.*, p. 223.

However, this was not because they were not professionally inclined, nor because they did not consider themselves professional. But they felt that others did not consider them professional. Specifically, they stated that (1) the public did not consider police work a profession; (2) that men in the department (white policemen) were not professionally inclined; and (3) that the department as a whole was the biggest obstacle to professionalization.

The policemen who reflect in their remarks professional role inclinations and self-images in a perceived nonprofessional milieu are in a dilemma. In attempting to reconcile their own claims to professional status as provided by the department's ideology, and the claims of others, they are placed in a position of role conflict. And this conflict is expressed in statements indicating uncertainty or ambivalence towards professionalism.

A review of some of the typical personal dilemmas from this group seems to be a crucial starting point for investigating the problems of the *Negro* policeman in the larger, white department. It is this context that makes it difficult, if not impossible, for police ideology to carry out its professional goals. It may seem ironical that the campaign of professionalism carried on by the department to bring about a strong work commitment, security, and personal and occupational pride, has in fact created insecurity, conflicts, tension, and questioning, for its ethnic minority members. For while the department has been successful in evoking a sense of commitment among these men, it has not been able to sway the public, nor has it been able to enlist the cooperation of its own majority membership in granting professional status to Negro policemen.

Here we may outline another sharp dilemma that confronts the Negro policeman in the acceptance of his role: the more professionalized he becomes, the greater the danger of his being cut off from his ethnic peers. To be a professional policeman, oriented to a police ideology, loyal to a police institution which values formality and values neutral practitioners, is to sacrifice some of his own ethnicity. The problem for him is how he can function in terms of the ideology of a police professional without neglecting the obligations he may also feel to his race, and the image he wishes to project outside of the police department.

Moreover, he also finds that when in certain situations he is treated as a policeman, the stigma that the role carries in the opinions of many members of minority groups becomes attached to him, and he is seen simply as a hated cop to be avoided, attacked, and even reviled as a traitor. Here the color of his skin is ignored. But when he is subject to what he terms as prejudices within the department, he has been metaphorically stripped of his uniform and exists only as a Negro. Thus his personal problem is to reconstitute himself as a whole man, transcending both his professional and ethnic roles. This problem does not exist for the white policeman who is externally free to merge his identity with that of his profession.

The Negro policeman considers himself a professional but cannot escape the judgment of the public about the nature of his occupation. The following policeman illustrated the need for public recognition as a reward for professional activity, a recognition not forthcoming.

> I guess you could say that the department is building toward a profession. They are stressing schooling on this job, and in the years ahead a high school diploma won't be enough. It is a profession, in that there are many elements of the police department involved that relate back to the individuals we serve . . . but people normally don't associate police work as a profession. I guess it's because of a case of familiarity—you see a policeman and you figure he is supposed to be there. It's not the type of job considered as being a white-collar job, like a doctor or a lawyer. But people don't know that policemen have to know some basic law. They are not doctors, but they have to know a certain amount of first aid.
>
> It can become a profession only if it is accepted by the public . . . Honestly, I don't think they ever will accept it as a profession. I think the public will accept the policeman as a civil servant—with the emphasis on servant. You have heard stories of people talking about how they pay their salaries. (12)

Such a response reflects ambivalence towards professionalism. The informant began with the belief that the department is building towards this goal, then went on to acknowledge that he himself considers it a profession, yet feels it is not considered as such by the public. This ambivalence was suggested by other policemen:

> I consider police work a profession and I also don't consider it a profession. The public itself will not accept it as such. Until the public is aware that it is, the ideas just will not be there. (38)

When this policeman was asked how he would define a profession, he took the opportunity of appraising the department in terms of its *failure* to live up to O. W. Wilson's (a police chief of California) well-intended statements of codifying the job along professional lines. Thus the realities of police work are viewed as inconsistent with professional intentions.

> The recruitment of policemen is not done as a profession does —education-wise and training-wise. And they [police department] with limited educational requirements and limited training requirements—and this limited training is not utilized by the department, or the public to make it a profession. They have been trying. The idea is there. O. W. Wilson sets up the idea—but it is not there. There are some men in the department who are dedicated to it. But until the public becomes aware of it as a profession, it won't be a profession. That is, the department won't get the budget allocation to carry out the ideas [Wilson's] to make it a profession . . . The policeman as a whole is not looked at as a person to help but is looked at as an enforcer of laws—and nobody likes an enforcer of laws—somebody to tell you what you can't do and what you should do. (38)

These policemen also referred to obstacles towards professionalism that exist within the membership of the department. Expectedly, they expressed the feeling that diverse opinions on professional views among the rank and file members and the professional association itself had led to tensions and conflicts. While differences between professional outlooks exist throughout the different organizational divisions, the focal point of conflict seems to revolve about those Negro policemen who work for the Youth Division. The following comments illustrate this.

Yes, a beautiful profession but we don't have professionals in it. The knowledge that you have to have to do an effective job and the image you have to project is a profession in that sense. I will give you an illustration. I was called into the job as a Youth Squad worker into the precinct. The lieutenant starts to ask me questions about police work. He asked me two questions. I gave him the answer just like that. But the job, although a prestige job, and you have to wear a white shirt and tie, you are looked upon as being social workers or frustrated detectives by the line people within the job. A college degree is required before you become a Youth worker. You are assigned to gangs. The work hours are good. We are unsung heroes. (19)

The police department dislikes the Youth Division because of its basic philosophy. So, being a Negro and in the Youth Division makes you subject to a double kind of attack. The Youth Organization was called the Crime Prevention Bureau forty years ago. And its purpose was to act as a buffer between the child and the court. In other words, when the child committed an offense, the officer would visit the home, discuss this with the parent and aid to prevent a recurrence of this. Now, the police department psychology has always been apprehension and arrest, not prevention. So you have this antithesis of ideas. In order to be proficient at this sort of thing, the Youth Division has always got men with the highest professional background as workers. This has caused other line organizations to sneer at them and refer to them as a bunch of sociologists. Whereas a line unit can show its measure of efficiency by the number of arrests and summonses it makes, the Youth unit can only show its effectiveness by the reduction of youthful crime in an area—which has been steadily rising for the past twenty years through no fault of the Youth Division, but due to the increase in population.

So, statistical-wise, the line organization can be more positive in displaying what they have accomplished than the Youth Division. So this gives the line organization fodder for their cannon, by maintaining they alone can help the problem and the Youth Division has no reason to exist. (18)

He continued:

Now, men have been promoted within line and within Youth units historically. So the fastest way to get ahead in the police department, once you pass the rank of captain, is to show a distinct aversion to the Youth units, vocally and politically. In other words, the captain wants to become an inspector. If he does, he stands a better chance of being an inspector if he throws in his philosophy of police work as being similar to the line unit's—arrest and apprehension. And also, if he openly shows disapproval of the Youth Units. Consequently, the Youth Division today has an inspector who wants to be promoted and who is busy engaged in neglecting the Youth Division, but actively engaged in fucking it up. (18)

Both of the above policemen feel that they are not accepted by the department because of the latter's punitive ideology, legitimized and sanctified by tradition, while they consider themselves to be committed to a treatment oriented, more humane ideology. While such a personal ideology of social amelioration may help to reassure the Negro policeman that he is not a "Kapo," it should also be said that because of his race, he is keenly aware and sensitive to the need for radical changes, and receptive to new courses of education and training instituted by the department for handling minority groups. Thus the Negro policeman uses this personal ideology not only to soften his role to avoid feelings of guilt, shame, or defensiveness, but is naturally responsive to the need for improved relations between the department and the ghetto. His professional orientation is not inconsistent with his minority group status; the realities of police work, however, are often incongruous with his professional orientations.

The tension and strains that exist between the ameliorative

orientation and the more traditional ideology are symbolized by the change in the law, which is a direct result of the civil rights movement. Thus diverse opinions arise as to how the police should react to the Negroes' demands for legal and social equality. As one policeman commented:

> The Supreme Court rule stated a search must be incident to an arrest. They made this binding on the law of the land. Illegal search and seizure is no good. The white cops say we have been hog-tied. I see this as having you present a better case. It enhances the job. Makes you a better cop. Makes you prepare a better case. The majority of white cops feel that this law is no good. The Negro cop doesn't think so because in actuality the law helps the minority groups and reduces differential treatment because of your color or neighborhood that you live in. If you live on 425 East 20th Street and the cops want to search you, they will knock on your door and ask you to open it up. If you don't open up there is nothing they can do. But on 132nd Street, if you don't open the door they will knock it down because they feel they can do this because of your race and because of the neighborhood. It means nothing to them. You are already presumed guilty because of your color and where you happen to live. The law insists that you take proper action regardless of race or neighborhood. This law wasn't made for me. But it's that ten feet tall cop who will abuse the laws. And this checks him! The same reasoning applies to the Civilian Review Board which checks the white cop knocking heads. This board is actually good for minority groups. It restricts the white cop from an arbitrary action and interpretation that he makes. (19)

As this policeman implies, ethical conduct is not just a matter of conforming to professional police norms. It is much more likely to be a matter of reconciling inconsistent norms. His own, as defined by police ideology, supported by law, and the Negro community, are to treat citizens uniformly. Those of his colleagues, as defined by the informal system of "police discretion," demand behavior that is supportive and cooperative. Thus in striving to conform to his own ideal of professional conduct, he runs the risk of violating his commitment to his colleagues who define the situation according to their own set of informal codes, or he may see other policemen violate his own professional standards which he has a personal and vested interest in maintaining because of pride in doing a professional job, and because his race values a law that is applied without favor. In sum, the Negro policeman may be considered unprofessional by his colleagues simply by conforming to the professionally prescribed ideal.

A number of policemen who considered themselves professionals expressed the feeling that the department failed to live up to its own standards. Specific charges were lip service in evaluating its personnel, and failure to apply universal standards of qualification for entrance to the department. The following quotation gives an example of this.

> If the police department lives up to standards that they are projecting it is a profession. But it is a two-way street. First they set a goal and in setting up this goal they don't live up to this goal. They have standards but only measured by the individuals they are dealing with. My standards would have to be high to get into a radio car. But another fellow who is white may have been on the job for only a few months and he gets a radio car. I can request to be a detective tomorrow morning and I would have to give my record to the reviewing board. But they would ask me only one question. Have you ever had any complaints from the department. Years ago when a Negro came into the department an old Irish sergeant would tell the Negro that he was going to give the Negro a complaint the following week. And he would give him his complaint. He knew in advance that he was going to give a complaint to the man because he was a Negro and for no other reason. (20)

Another policeman, after stressing his own professional aspirations, noted the following obstacles to professionalism.

> [The department] does have a chance to become professionalized providing we have the right personnel in the department and properly trained. There is a big to-do now about kids

74

attending school. They are hoping to get more of the police officers to attend police courses. In order to do this though, they would have to offer more incentive to the men to go to school. I am now attending the Police Academy for these courses. When you go back a bit, I think we are placed in the same position as the military service in this regard—when the service was recruiting guys to fight in the war—and at that time, the U.S. government was not particularly interested in the kinds of guys they were recruiting for the services. They wanted to win the war. Same thing applies here, even though the police department has a very thorough investigative procedure, especially against Negro candidates. They really go out of their way to check Negro candidates who come into the job. They say it isn't true, but I am quite sure that there is a quota system at work for the Negro who comes into the job. Let's face it, they average about twenty-five Negroes on a list of candidates who come into the job. That's not many. (15)

Such a response strongly implies that Negroes are treated differently from whites when applying to the department. As a side point, however, we doubt that standards are in fact more stringent for Negro than for white candidates at the present time. They may have been more strictly enforced for Negroes who joined the force five or ten years ago before competition for educated Negroes in private industry became prevalent. Although this cannot be supported by any conclusive statistical data, a number of policemen were inclined to disagree with the police officer quoted above; they felt it was relatively easy to become a policeman, white or Negro. It is difficult to get an adequate number of Negro policemen to master the paper and pencil work needed for admission to the force, perhaps because there is a historical educational deficit in the Negro community. In fact, the department seems to relax standards to recruit Negro policemen because of the political and economic advantages (see Chapter 2) in so doing. Even though there may be no discrimination in recruiting men, the Negro may feel discriminated against by the entrance and promotion tests. It might be held that discrimination is implied in such tests because of the deficient performance of Negroes on paper and pencil tests, as witness the recent discussion of the inadequacy of pencil-and-paper intelligence test results for Negro children.

Repudiation of professional status

When asked whether or not they considered police work as a profession, ten Negro policemen answered in the negative. In contradiction to the previously discussed group which shows ambivalence toward professional status (including awareness of the conflict between their positive professional orientation and the obstacles in the way of their achieving such status), the present group evinces a different reaction. One finds in their answers a lack of identification with the department, little involvement in it, and a denial of any claims it may have to being professional. While it is difficult to establish causes with the information at our disposal, an analysis of their reasons shows that it is possible that these men entered the police force with a willingness to accept the professional ideology, but that subsequent experiences led to their rejection of it. Moreover, this view is held equally by both groups described in Chapter 2, those who had a police orientation at the time they entered civil service and those who had no specific commitment to police work as such but who were induced to join merely for economic reasons and reasons of security. Both now have a negative attitude towards the department, the functions it fulfills and its personnel.

> I don't think it will ever become a profession . . . The men in the police department limit it in becoming a profession. You don't have a strong enough code of ethics. Morally, not even ready to become a profession. What requirements do they have anyhow? What requirements other than sound health, and good character which is vague. I didn't even study a day to get into the department—to get the job. There is no preparation. You can't go to school unless you're prepared—to become a doctor or a teacher. You have to meet requirements and you just don't have this on the job. You have some standards now in the Police Academy—and now they're thinking of this college, but many of the requirements are

76

not mandatory. You must not forget this either. And that's the element in the department. Many of them are not suitable to be ragpickers. This idea of police brutality. There is a lot of justification for this. (4)

It is evident from this critical appraisal that professionalism is an illusory goal, since the men in the department are perceived as incompetent and dishonorable. A true profession can be said to exist when it guarantees to the public not only the competence of its personnel but also their honor.

Another policeman expressed his disavowal of professional status in different terms, yet it is indicative of the strain felt by Negro policemen who were not initially disposed to police work when they joined the service. The negative attitudes they felt were confirmed after entering the department.

> The police department thinks it is a profession. They try to make it a professional job. They try to get more and more educated men in this job. But let's put it this way. You wouldn't expect a college graduate to become a policeman when he has to deal with derelicts, dope addicts. Some of us live with these types of people. And I might run into an instance where you get a disorderly person and I try to reason with him and I get no response. I might have to resort to a little physical force, not outright brutality, but a little force. And you find yourself being reprimanded by some Joe Schmo sergeant. Now I know what I'm doing. But he comes along and gives me a reprimand for what I did. Why does a college guy want to put up with this John Q. Public? He can go into private industry . . . Like I said, it takes a smart Negro and a dumb white to come on this job. The Negro just doesn't have much of a choice. (36)

Even the police oriented are found to repudiate professional claims:

> They say it is a profession. But I don't feel it is a profession. A profession is being paid for your talents. A cop is in between both ends. The people are on one end and the bosses on the

other end. The bosses are interested in statistics, that's what makes them happy—they want action. The sergeant is on your back, the lieutenant is on his back, the captain is on his back, all the way up to the top. The job will never become a profession until the bosses put aside their statistics and become interested in people. Then you can do a job to the best of your ability. (8)

Other policemen made the same point.

As far as I am concerned a profession means more understanding of people. You have three or four different types of cops. You have one type who understands people—you have one who tries to understand people—and you have (most of them) one who just doesn't care about people. He goes by the rule book and just doesn't think . . . Right here in Brownsville, the biggest problem is that most of the cops have no interest in people at all. In addition to this, the department has no facilities to acquaint them with people, to get interested in people. (14)

GOOD AND BAD COPS

To be successful in police work, policemen are required to have the necessary skills, psychological attributes, and personal qualities to do a good professional job. A description of these qualities, on the whole, substantiates the professional claim for the department, but focuses on what is proper and desirable behavior on the part of policemen so that one may evaluate the manner in which the work is to be done. Negro policemen, regardless of their responses to professionalism, characterized "good" policemen in the following general terms: (1) a person who knows the job, is educated, trained, and has knowledge of the law; (2) a policeman who cares about people; (3) one who has possession of ethical qualities such as integrity, humility, and fidelity; (4) one who can perform multiple skills in response to different community needs;

and (5) a person who has a well-organized personality, and is in control of the tempo of his reactions.

A selection of some of the typical characteristics of "good" policemen will follow. However, since all policemen cited combinations of qualities, it is difficult to determine which are crucial for professional police practice. A "good" policeman is:

> One who knows his job. I have no use for a policeman who has been in the department as long as I have been and doesn't know his job. The ignorant policeman I'm talking about. This is the guy who will cause trouble. I have no use for a stupid cop. (16)

> A well-integrated personality. Secondly, a man should be—as long as he is basically a sound thinking man. Then, he should be an educated person. Again, we have gotten away from de's, dem's, and dose policemen, if you want to put it that way. I think the man (aside from his own personal development and personality) should be one of integrity. (39)

> A policeman who tries to understand the particular problems in the community that he works. Who tries to hold himself not to discredit the department or himself. Who puts himself in the job where he puts himself in a good light. Where young people will respect him and emulate him. (37)

A good policeman can refer to both those who are professionally inclined and identify with police work as a career, and those who just consider it a job. As one policeman remarked:

> There are several good cops. One who says that being a policeman is a way of life. The other who says being a policeman is a job. Both of these guys can be good cops, but both can be bad cops. But primarily a good cop is one who is primarily a good person. It is probably the best thing that one policeman can say to another—that he is a good cop. It's the highest compliment one can pay to another officer on the job. (34)

One policeman felt that a steady post brings about a good policeman. He noted:

> A steady post and a good cop go hand in hand. When you have a steady post you get to know the neighbors, the people in the neighborhood and potential trouble spots, and consequently, you begin to understand the problems and the reason why. (30)

This is an interesting point. For in the absence of intimate, personal contacts, the opinions of the community regarding the policeman tend to be determined almost wholly by the stereotype of the cop. The variable, time on the beat, is a crucial factor in allowing the policeman the opportunity of asserting his personal interpretation of the police role, while at the same time removing from himself the stigma of the occupation.

The policeman just quoted went on to mention other qualities of the good policeman.

> A good cop is one who can keep a steady or level head. One who can check his temper and knows a policeman's job well enough (arrests and summonses) . . . Today, a good cop has to know how to talk to people . . . I've found out that the cop who knew how to say hello got along. But the majority of the policemen, especially the white policemen, didn't have respect for other people. They talk to the Negro this way: "Hey you, get over here." Or, they might say, "I'll stick this stick up your black ass." Now, I have seen policemen who are very stern but who would say, "Mister, I'm warning you. One more time that's all." And you might have a crowd around you but you didn't have the crowd talking about brutality, even though you were stern, but you weren't disrespectful to the person. But other policemen just don't know how to talk. They treat the Negro like he is scum—like he is nothing. And it's that way of talking, that attitude that gets people mad. (30)

This same policeman suggested that not understanding the law is the cause for such disrespect.

> A good policeman is a policeman who knows the fundamen-
> tals of the law. A lot of policemen push people around be-
> cause they don't know the fundamentals of the law—because
> they don't know what to do. And because they don't know
> what to do, the easiest thing for them is to push and that
> solves the problem. But they don't think. (30)

A superior officer added another dimension to the above comments. It is not enough to have knowledge of the law, one must
understand the "spirit of the law."

> I am one who doesn't believe that the law should be enforced
> to the letter. The spirit of the law should govern most Su-
> preme Court officers. The spirit of the law is what we need.
> On the other hand, I don't think we should become social
> workers. The policeman with common sense will know when
> to enforce the law to the letter and when to invoke the spirit
> of the law . . . We should give warnings in many cases and
> not make arrests simply to make an arrest. The police manual
> provides for this invoking of the spirit of the law. (41)

The negative image of the profession is the stereotype of the
"bad" policeman, one whose incompetence is matched by his
insensitivity, brutality, and bigotry. The "bad" policeman typifies
all those qualities that these Negro policemen avoid. He is the
negative model, has no understanding of minority groups, shows
favoritism, and is feared. In sum, he incorporates all the racist
attitudes of some white policemen.

> I don't believe a good policeman is one who shows favoritism
> or one who expects certain things, or expects a certain stand-
> ard of conduct from certain types of people. In other words,
> one who feels (and this is most important) all Negroes are
> the same, or all Jews are the same, or all Puerto Ricans are
> the same. And I feel most colored policemen feel this the
> most. Because this leads to an attitude of looking down upon
> people. (21)

Another policeman openly directed his attack at the Irish
policeman.

81

You get some policemen—you narrow down to Irish—who are very officious. They go with the attitude that if you go through the red light this is something you have done to them personally. They are very raw and blunt. They are extremely uncouth. They have no savvy in the way they talk to people, handle people. They have complete disregard for other people's feelings, and will start beating on people without any bit of provocation. (32)

He went on to remark:

A couple of guys I knew as kids are now cops. They are more or less oddballs of the crowd. We are going to have a party tonight and are going to invite Joe Blow. He is a dead-beat. All the guys who had dealings with him found him to be afraid of people. He always had a dog with him. A real vicious dog. Around the time that he became a cop you could see his whole attitude change as the police badge replaced this dog. So the badge becomes more or less his crutch in the world, and the dog was his crutch when he was a kid. There are a lot of guys like that. You could tell he was always the kind who got beat up in the block. These guys make some very rough cops! (32)

Equally "bad" is the policeman who "stands behind his shield." The outcome is the same, however.

The pushers, the sadist, the shield man. The policeman who stands behind his shield, and because he has a shield he thinks he has the right to push people around. But you should stand in front of your shield. You have white policemen in Harlem who say, "Get away from me, kid," or, he might say, "I bet you don't have any father the way you act." This kind of policeman takes his uniform off and what does he do. He looks for some black woman in Harlem. He wants to get a piece. But he puts his uniform on and Harlem is no good, it's crummy, it's dirty, the people are no good. You see what I mean? (30)

Another policeman leveled off at the John Birch policeman.

> The guy who puts on a uniform and becomes 10 feet tall.
> A guy who changes, one guy as a cop and another guy as an
> individual. I've got a guy in my office (he is white). This
> guy is a dummy. He identifies with the John Birch Society.
> Yet, he can't properly make out a report to this day. He
> turns in a bad report and when it is turned back to him he
> says the boss is a Negro and that is why it was turned back
> to him. (19)

In summary, the advocates of professionalism reflect in their
remarks the publicly stated ideology of the police department,
and act to propagate the image of service to the community, high
ideals, and noble ends. This ideology constitutes their self-
definition, and functions to develop personal and occupational
pride, and security in the face of a public that is not convinced.

Notwithstanding the actual and potential aspects of these self-
definitions, the uncertain or ambivalent responses to them as well
as the outright repudiation of professional claims, allow us to
separate sermonizing from reality and to discover the point
where distortions, misrepresentations, and outright fictions begin
to emerge. These policemen were instrumental in pointing to
those aspects of the institutional framework of the job and of the
community context of their work, which function to limit and
contradict professional role performance, and serve as a framework for subsequent discussion. Factors that were mentioned included: (1) the influence exercised on the activities of police work
by the public's image of it; (2) the service orientation of the
police which is not reflected in its dealings with the Negro community; (3) that one's colleagues do not in fact conform to certain professional standards of conduct, nor are many of them
competent practitioners of the police art; (4) the delinquency of
the department in upholding its responsibility for providing
theoretical and practical training in community relations and
further understanding of minority groups; and (5) the discovery
that at times the department pays only lip service to the ideal of

equality of recognition for Negro policemen both in terms of qualification standards for entrance, and in terms of assignments and promotions. In large part then, the reality of police work for the policeman threatens and in some instances destroys his identification with professionalism. It is one thing to consider oneself in professional terms; it is another to transcend one's professional role. The Negro is a member of a racial minority group as well as of an occupational one.

4

The Negro policeman and his white counterpart

The dilemma of the Negro policeman resides in the dual position that he occupies and the two essential roles that he plays. Some of the social and cultural conditions which give rise to this dilemma have been discussed. Although there is no logical contradiction between being a Negro and a policeman, the fact is, that the Negro policeman often views his situation as contradictory and inconsistent.

This chapter will pursue this theme by focusing on the interpersonal relationship of white and Negro policemen as seen from the point of view of Negro policemen. Its general concern is with the way these men conceptualize their occupation, how they

85

view the white policeman, and the manner in which they feel he views them.

The chapter also considers the social and administrative arrangements which maintain a level of cooperation between white and Negro policemen in the face of personal inclinations that go in contrary directions. While police work can be carried out alone, it is seen as necessary, desirable, and expedient that Negro and white policemen work together. However, the relationship that unites the two in mutual dependence does not necessarily negate a pattern of white superiority and condescension. Thus we will be concerned with two levels of meaning: the objective requirements of interdependence, and the subjective intentions and meanings that white and Negro police give to these requirements.

Lastly, a Negro policeman, while hoping to be accepted as a policeman by his white "brother officer," at the same time undergoes social discrimination that impresses upon him in concrete terms his status as a partial outsider. Not only does he feel that *white* policemen are prejudiced and discriminate against him, but that the department as a whole does as well. And he may feel that this operates at all levels—in recruitment, promotion, and assignments.

THE NEGRO POLICEMAN IN HIS PROFESSIONAL ROLE

The job as a basis of cooperation

When asked the question, "What do white policemen think of Negro policemen?" many of the forty-one Negro policemen reported that they were viewed as policemen on the job. In other words, white policemen do not openly acknowledge differences among Negro and white policemen on the job. The nature of their work, and the similarity of function, generates a form of mutual dependence. On the job the Negro and white policeman need each other. Most of these men, however, felt that little social intercourse existed outside the job. The situation was described in this way:

> As long as you are working side by side you treat each other as policemen. You act in a professional manner. But ten minutes after 4:00 P.M., the majority of the white cops go their way and the Negro cop goes his way. (16)

Even when a Negro police officer participates in social gatherings, he is not completely accepted. In such situations, he may bring a friend along so he won't feel so uncomfortable. In addition, the potential dangers in the situation require the company of a fellow Negro colleague; for should the party transform itself, as some parties will, into an exchange of racial slurs, it is desirable to have a friend of the same race there.

> It's wonderful in the station house. We are going to apprehend this criminal together—wonderful. We are going to do police work together—wonderful. But off duty, that's different. It's funny. When you walk into a room full of white cops getting together for a few drinks with their wives, there's a very cold feeling. (20)

Another policeman reflected on the difficulty in knowing the true feelings of the white police officer. The implication was that there might be a discrepancy between the white policeman's behavior toward him and how he actually feels. Nevertheless, he made the same point—that the job of being a policeman requires cooperation, regardless of personal likes, dislikes, prejudice, or discrimination.

> I don't know. They may tell you one thing but mean another. It's a hard question. As a Negro I know how a Negro feels. But I have to be white to know what whites feel of Negro patrolmen. Like I say, when you work in the uniform you are brothers. But out of uniform it's a different story. When in uniform the white man needs me and I need him. You've got to help one another. You may save my life and I may save your life. Out of uniform I don't know whether I will save your life and I don't know what you will do. (28)

When asked whether he was convinced that the white police-man would come to his aid during working hours, this policeman commented on the need for self-protection which becomes the basis of cooperation. This common dependence was expressed in the following terms.

> There is no problem about whether he will come to my aid. This is the necessity of the job. The job you hold makes it a fraternalistic dependence. Like I say, you work by yourself as one and patrol vast areas, a minimum of six blocks. You are there by yourself. And if you need aid, he will come to you and you will go to him. There is a definite dependence, and race and color don't enter the fact. You know if this wasn't so, the whole structure of the thing would fall apart. There may be resentment but you have got to help one an-other. (28)

In addition to the job which requires both parties to respond to each other as policemen, the element of racial etiquette is implied in all previous remarks. No word or phrase which empha-sizes racial differences or can otherwise be taken as a sign of racial prejudice is allowed. We would assume that there is mutual agreement in the deletion of potentially controversial language from conversations between Negro and white policemen. All policemen probably sense what would be acceptable and what would produce anxiety in a biracial context. The greater the hostility between Negro and white policemen, the greater the need for some self-conscious avoidance of taboo areas for the sake of work efficiency.

The view of common enemies as the basis of cooperation

Interdependence as a basis for developing sympathetic responses of whites and Negroes to each other as policemen results from the common struggle against the enemy of the police department, the criminal and the public. In the company of other policemen one can receive support and comfort in the face of the "public enemy." The primary group allows the individual patrolman to feel a lessening of the stigma attached to his office in the public's mind, and offers an element of safety in the face of criminal acts.

> To me, it's a funny thing about being a policeman. A guy in my office I know he is a bigot. I have told him so. But if anyone should attack him I would go to his aid. I would hope he would come to my aid if I was in trouble. You have to stick together for self-protection and self-preservation. They say strength in unity against the common enemy. The public! (22)

Expediency as a basis of cooperation

A few policemen expressed the feeling that their fellow officers responded to them as policemen because of the administrative advantages accruing to them and to the department as a whole of having Negro policemen on the job. The mechanism of self-interest is particularly well exemplified by the following remarks.

> It has been my experience that the white policemen have a very high opinion of Negro policemen. Of course, I think there are a lot of reasons this is so. One thing, by and large, Negro police officers are assigned to predominantly Negro areas and this increases his effectiveness because he has greater rapport with people working there than the white policeman. He is also able to come by more information than the white police officer is able to come by. (24)

Ironically, such views suggest that the Negro policeman is recognized as a policeman to the extent that he can be used as a Negro. He can make claims to police status in direct proportion to his access to information in Negro areas. The notion is that the Negro police officer understands the symbols and meanings of Negroes who live in the ghetto, and can deal with them more effectively than the white policeman.[1]

---

[1] The use of the Negro policemen in the terms we have described has its parallel in Hughes' concept of the "straw boss." See Everett C. Hughes, "Ethnic Relations in Industry and Society," in Sigmund Noscow and William H. Form, eds., *Man, Work, and Society* (New York, Basic Books, Inc., 1962), p. 564.

Another policeman described how he introduces white policemen into the special eccentricities of ghetto life, which are crucial to administrative success. Here the Negro policeman becomes a sort of guide, attuning the colonial administration to the ways of the native population.

> I have in this neighborhood four or five white cops who I introduced to Brownsville. If you are a good cop and show him what he has to do, and if he listens, he is successful and none of the cops had any trouble. This neighborhood became a training ground or training school for the white cop . . . In a neighborhood like this, most of the white cops like to work with the Negro officer. If the Negro cop is good everything works out all right. If the white cop is the brutal type and irresponsible, then things don't work out and it's a waste. (14)

Another policeman, who obviously relishes the white policeman's dependence on him in his own territory, decried the changes in his relationship with the white policeman when he has learned the ropes.

> Unless he has been closely associated with a Negro officer, it's the way he feels about Negroes in general. I come into contact with white police detectives who are friendly. When they need me to teach them and get them started they were friendly. But after they learned the ropes they didn't want to have anything to do with you. That's some—but there are others who still come to me for advice. They will still come back to me after I have trained them or helped them. (33)

Special requirements for working with whites

One policeman outlined an ironic situation—to establish himself as a policeman in the eyes of his white counterpart, the Negro must do more than is required of him. The implication is that acceptance as a good cop is contingent upon making oneself indispensible to the particular organizational unit to which one is assigned.

I remember when I first came to the precinct, everybody ran away from the switchboard. It was a little complicated. If you made a mistake and you got a call from a superior officer, it could be your head. I took over the switchboard many times. Being nosey, I asked questions about the board, and I would consequently help other policemen when they needed help on the board. I also learned something about administrative procedures. I learned these procedures through trial and error. I asked a lieutenant a thousand questions a day but he never became disgusted with me. Why? Because this means you are interested in the job . . . There were a couple of fellows who didn't care for me—they would come into the office to see if I had anything over (work) for them. What would I do? I would do my work completely, but I would also do some of their work. I wasn't supposed to do this. They were shocked by this. They said: You're all right. This meant an hour savings on their part. (13)

As this policeman points out, through his work he gradually constructed a set of favorable personal impressions while at the same time decreasing the stereotypical view that white policemen may hold of the Negro policemen as a group. However, we must be careful not to overstate these special requirements for working with white policemen, for there is no clear evidence in the quotation that suggests it is his racial status that causes him to do more than is required in the situation.

THE POLICEMAN AS A NEGRO POLICEMAN

The largest number of policemen felt they were viewed primarily as Negroes. But although they were viewed as Negroes, they were considered "different from the rest." The Negro policeman is viewed as "different" because he is a member of the high order of the police fraternity. He is acceptable to the police group because he is a "professional cop." We would observe that this "exception" category is typical for Negro Americans in the initial phase of socialization. He is a "white" Negro. By so conceiving him, the white policeman allows a Negro to serve in his role. It also allows white policemen to retain their prejudice toward other Negro policemen who are not his work partners, and against Negroes in general. However, even this category of response is dubious since Negro policemen are subject to probable repudiation and insult in their struggle to acquire professional prestige and job mobility, and to overcome the repudiation and insults directed against their ethnic peers. The following responses attest to this view.

> He thinks this: You are a good nigger. You are different, he says. You are one of us. But that in itself is a lot of bullshit. We are not like them and they sure as hell are not like us. (37)

> He feels that the Negro policeman is an exception and that the others are different. I think there exists a genuine regard and respect for their ability to do a job and get a job done. But they are slow to trust beyond ones they know, that is if they don't know another Negro. And when they don't know another Negro they seem to go back to a sense of fear, and out of fear comes hate. (31)

THE NEGRO POLICEMAN AS A NEGRO

A minority of the men interviewed felt that white policemen responded to them simply in terms of racial categories and attributed to the Negro policeman all the stigmas implied by racial prejudice. In this situation, the white policeman completely accepts the stereotyped response to Negroes, and the uniform of the Negro policeman does not in any way change these feelings. The following comments illustrate this.

> He thinks of him as a Negro and this is brought out in his actions. In much of his speech he brings this out about how he feels about the Negro policeman. No liberal person has to

tell me how many Negro friends he has. No right-thinking person has to tell me that he is for the Negro. The fact that Ralph Bunche and other Negroes have made it, well, Ralph Bunche still can't eat in Mississippi. (19)

The thought he has, I suppose, are the things he was told and brought up with about Negroes. Here he finds himself having to work with Negroes 24 hours a day and yet, his white make-up makes him foreign to Negroes. And I think working with us is confusing to him and making him upset. He works with us but then he goes back to his white neighborhood. He kind of lives in these two worlds. On the one hand he works with us because he has no choice. It's like the service. You can't stand a guy's guts. But if he is in trouble you say it could have been me. I think it is the nature of the job that holds us together. The need for each other is there. (38)

A modification of this theme is to taboo the whole area of race. This is the classic example of treating the Negro as an "invisible man." In this connection, the white policeman might say that the less he notices him the better it is. By ignoring the Negro as much as possible the white policeman removes himself from contact with him, and this lack of interaction relieves the white police officer from expressing hostility against the Negro policeman. However, this does not work, for situations do occur which require interaction. Consequently, the white police officer must fall back on other social devices to isolate himself from his own hostility. One policeman talked about the desire of white policemen to avoid contact while at the same time being forced to come to terms with the Negro policeman.

I think they are a bit confused about the Negro policemen because most of them would rather not consider us at all. This is because of their background. Those who do consider us, at this point, are rather confused. The Negro realizes how difficult it is to get anything in this job except through promotions. The white policeman will look at you as a Negro and asks how did you get there. They are a little disoriented

93

because of the trend of Negroes who are training, working hard going to school. We are going to get promoted. We don't have enough bosses. The Guardian Association is more outspoken. So the white policeman is confused because he doesn't know where the Negroes' loyalties lie, and the fact that Negroes are active in improving themselves. (34)

ISSUES THAT EVOKE LATENT HOSTILITY

In answering the question of how they were viewed by white policemen, a few policemen found it necessary to refer to certain types of issues as support for their answers. Basically, they were responded to as Negroes or "exceptions" and the issues confirmed this. For example, one policeman talked about the John Birch infiltration of the police department. He felt that if a white policeman were a Birchite he must dislike Negroes, because Birchites dislike Negroes.

> . . . they look at the Negro cop as an oddity. How did he get on the job? He has a hell of a nerve wanting to be a cop, they say. That is the sort of thing. So the Negro who works in this department gets the feeling that he is working for the John Birch Society. Isn't that a hell of a note? (18)

Why does he get this feeling?

> Because the history of police political thought has always been conservative. A white cop doesn't make enough money to fall into an upper middle income group, but his life style is oriented to the upper middle income group. That is, because he makes too much money to fall into the low income group. So as a political group he stretches and reaches for the conservative element in government and politics and actually thinks along these lines. This may account for strong hints and prejudices also in the department. Where he is friendly with the Negro cop, the attitude is this: You are

different, Jim. You are not like the rest of them, Jim. You are not like the rest of them son-of-a-bitches out there. That out there may be my family but he never thinks of that. (18)

When a Negro talks with a Negro opinions may vary on issues as much as when a white talks with a white. Tensions result and as the heat of the argument intensifies they stop to avoid further argument. Because Negro and white must work together, they avoid such issues. In this regard, another policeman talked about two other issues considered relevant by Negro policemen: the civil rights movement, and the civilian review board.

I think they like a quiet, inarticulate Negro who will go along with the program (that is, one who gets along with other policemen) type of policeman. I think they are hostile toward the outspoken Negro police officer, usually because the outspoken Negro officer is better informed on civil rights and is not afraid to speak out and will not ignore criticism. This creates resentment of the person and fear. The fear comes from the fact that this officer supports the movement out on the street that he is out to contol from the point of view of law. But I feel this apprehension is baseless. I feel their anxiety (white policemen) is baseless. When you come down to it, the officer, if law is violated, will take action no matter what color he is. I have known CORE policemen to arrest CORE demonstrators. Matter of fact one policeman I know whose wife is in the group (CORE group). I think this is proof of supporting the law and proof that this anxiety is baseless—the feeling that the Negro policeman supports the demonstrations. He can support the demonstration and also enforce the law. On the other hand, speaking with more informed white police officers, they have a different attitude. They accept the fact of the civil rights movement as such, but they concern themselves with the kind of civilian review board, not whether they are going to have one, and he sees the Negro officer as an individual, and judges them accordingly. This approach is held by one white police officer out of ten. (39)

The "quiet, inarticulate Negro who goes along with the program," is one who tacitly shares the "ethical" norms of conduct, belief, and valuation of the police world as defined by the white majority. He is rewarded by being considered a "good Negro policeman." The one who speaks out rocks the boat, and in the eyes of his fellow officers leaves himself open to the charge of ambiguous loyalty. The *modus operandi* for cooperation is to say nothing about the civil rights movement or other issues contrary to the dominant police line.

Another policeman, making the same point, went on to discuss an incident which illustrates an attempt on the part of white policemen to prevent conflict from rising to the surface.

> When things come into the papers (NAACP was talking about police brutality)—I had taken the papers inside into the office. I went to the bathroom and when I came back the office is very quiet. One guy looks at me and says: I'm sorry. I say to him: What are you talking about? He says: You didn't hear me? Then two and two came together. I knew what they were talking about. They fail to realize this is a human problem not just a Negro problem. They hold themselves above the people they work with and above the people in the neighborhood. I feel there is such a gap between the Negro and white cop. When we have straightened out the whole civil rights movement, then perhaps, there may be a comrade feeling. The civil rights movement has now brought to the front all the attitudes of prejudice that they have been carrying around with them all these years. For example: they bring out some news clipping from the *Journal-American* or the *News* with some anti-Negro column or article and they post it on the bulletin board. (15)

In sum, all Negro policemen were aware of the racial boundaries separating them from their police status, and this is highlighted by those policemen who were considered as Negro "exceptions," or simply "Negroes." Such categories of "acceptance" strongly imply an inequality that exists at the level of interpersonal rela-

tions. Let us now turn to the manner in which the Negro policeman views the white policeman.

THE NEGRO POLICEMAN VIEWS THE WHITE POLICEMAN

The majority of these men had negative images of white policemen. White policemen were viewed as brutal, incompetent, lazy,
ultraconservative, and bigoted. In fact, the negative model of the
policeman defined by these Negro policemen in their discussion
of police professionalism, for the most part, characterizes, for
them, the white cop. Furthermore, this group, to a substantial
degree, is made up of civil service oriented policemen. The negative images they have of white policemen now are consistent with
their earlier views of whites who become policemen. The following
statements are typical for this group.

> Well, first of all, I figure their educational level—with some
> exceptions—is not too high. And I don't find they are too en-
> lightened. I feel that, unless they had a job like the police
> department, these whites would for the most part be bus
> drivers, and performing menial tasks elsewhere. (29)

The white policeman is also viewed as "immoral."

> Several years ago I belonged to a club. It was a social club of
> Negro cops and correction men. We gave a dance one night.
> One of the fellows at the club has a tendency to go overboard
> —he was loaded. He had to do an eight to four tour of duty.
> The dance was over at 3:00 A.M. He passed a couple of lights
> after the dance was over. He was stopped by two white cops.
> He was nasty so they booked him into the station house.
> While he's in the station house getting booked, a cop is out-
> side propositioning his wife who stayed behind in the car.
> Meanwhile, in the station house he realized he was wrong
> and everything was passed over. Two days later, after the inci-

dent, his wife tells him about the white cop who proposi-
tioned her. That's the way they are. (15)

The cliché of the white policeman as being discourteous to
Negro citizens, or neglecting his police duty in the ghetto, is seen
as real. The white policeman uses a standard of justice that treats
a Negro-upon-Negro assault as something less serious than
a Negro-upon-white assault. White policemen are also considered
guilty of assaulting Negro prisoners, and are accused of using
abusive language in their dealings with Negroes.

> I have witnessed white policemen abusing prisoners . . . I feel
> that the prisoner before his arrest may have created this
> [antagonism] but after having the handcuffs on I have wit-
> nessed white policemen beating these men. I have seen this.
> I have heard the white policeman call the Negro violator a
> black mother-fucker, and black this and black that. And I
> have had to constantly remind these officers that I, too, am
> Negro. (37)

> The attitude of the white cop is horrible toward the Negro.
> My neighborhood, the neighborhood I work in, has changed
> from white to Negro and Puerto Rican. In this neighborhood
> you find the white cop who is quick with his hands and with
> his mouth. He is ready to call you a spic in a hurry. The
> white cops have all sorts of ways of abusing a guy—I mean
> oral abuse. As you ride through the street, every time you see
> a radio car which has pulled over a civilian car, 90 times out
> of 100, the radio car has pulled over a Negro guy or a Negro
> couple. It doesn't matter what the neighborhood is, white or
> Negro. (15)

A large number of these men indicated that white policemen
were ultraconservative and bigoted. And a few Negro policemen
offered an explanation for this. The following answers are typical.

> Most of them are narrow minded, bigoted and opinionated,
> middle class in their thinking. Their scope and thinking is
> geared to the nineteenth century, to one-horse towns, to some

98

other kind of world that just isn't there. They are ultra-conservative . . . Most of this comes from their upbringing . . . And I think it is their religious training. I believe it is Catholicism that keeps them so opinionated . . . A feudal kind of mind is passed on to these people. (38)

The white cop believes that he represents a cross section of America . . . He doesn't see this as being one job . . . When he identifies with the ultraconservatives and their cause, and the John Birch Society, this only adds to his problem . . . And this is the only reason why you can see in the precincts notices . . . inviting all white Protestant members of the police department to join the White Citizens Council of New York. (19)

The Negro policeman is also not happy with the dual standards that are applied to membership in outside ideological organizations.

Another thing: there is in my office in Youth never at any time a remote thought of any kid joining a Muslim sect. The investigations are really complete. But I've yet to see a similar investigation of a group called the SPONGE [The Society for the Prevention of Negroes from Getting Everything]. I know five guys who are members. There has been no attempt to investigate them! A Negro is investigated to infinity. Heaven help him if he is a member of a Muslim sect. But not the white cop. You have to be a magician to hide anything from the investigators. By the way there are no Negro investigators. (19)

This typical collection of negative reactions to white policemen could easily have been made by Negro civilians or sectors of the white public which hold substantially similar negative images of policemen. Many Negro policemen thus appear to identify with their ethnic group and accept the minority community's image of white police as well as other relevant issues affecting the lives of such members, even though there is a strong likelihood that such views are not easily expressed, if at all, within the department.

They are involved, as a group, in the Negro community per se, and identify their own future in the department with that of the community. They have come to see that collective action in civil rights outside of the department is necessary, and this helps support and maintain their own values and interests inside the department. They are Negroes as well as policemen. In addition, their attachment to the Negro community may give them personal support and reassurance in the face of tensions and personal conflicts that arise because they are policemen.

Lastly, it is not inconsistent to point out that the majority of those Negro policemen who felt that white policemen treated them as exceptions or simply as black boys in blue suits are among this group. This could suggest that there is a kind of reinforcement of racial ideologies at work between whites and Negroes on the force. The mutual reinforcement of racist attitudes at the same time brings into play mechanisms that prevent them from becoming overt.

A second group of policemen were ambivalent in their responses to the white police. In this group (representing a minority of responses) discussion of white policemen fluctuated between an apology for and a criticism of their behavior. Substantively, they tend to treat the white policemen as unfortunate victims of a deficient upbringing who need, like children, to be understood. One must feel sorry for them rather than hate them. This group is made up, on the whole, of police oriented policemen.

> I hate to categorize white policemen as such. I happen to know many good white policemen, even some working in Negro neighborhoods. And I have known some that are prejudiced. I do feel however that the same anxieties and prejudices that exist with the police department have no connection with the department, but are problems which carry over from the policeman's civilian life. I don't believe a policeman changes when he takes the job. (26)

> Some of them go to greater lengths to smooth over a situation than Negro cops. On the other hand, you have a core of white

policemen who have no sense of dedication or responsibility to the community. (39)

The Negro policeman in this group has the need to express and assert himself as a Negro while trying to create a viable working relationship with white policemen. This results in an accommodation to the attitudes of white policemen towards themselves, a process of developing temporary working agreements between the two. What Sumner called "antagonist cooperation" could be the term that best describes this relationship. Apologetic and critical feelings alternate, as indicated in the following quotations.

> They are good policemen. They do their job just like the Negro policemen. Everyone has biases and prejudices. This you can't eradicate. But you should be impartial when you do a job. I have no ill feeling against white policemen. But when they put on the uniform they should represent all the people. Some white policemen do represent all the people and some don't. I guess the ones that don't are in the minority. (28)

> I feel they are conscientious. I feel they do an excellent job, police-wise. They are head and shoulders above any police group in the country. They have more knowledge, more facts, and more honesty. However, they still have a long way to go in learning that there are two types of people in every race, good and bad. And they must not be lumped together as I say. To boil it down in simplest terms—the white race is not superior to any colored race, and racial intermarriage is not the end of the world. In other words, they have the same prejudice which is found in any group involving race. Although they try to hide it, it's still there. (21)

The above policemen who practice accommodation are not at war with the department but are adapting to the behavior of their fellow officers who are in many ways conducting themselves in an "unprofessional" manner. The ambivalence they reflect is a result of their expectations of what their brother officers should be, and awareness that the expectations are being disappointed. They object to colleagues who behave in a stereotypical way and act out all that is bad in the police image. It is at this point that the Negro policeman's latent identity as a Negro becomes manifest; for such white transgressions are the expression of prejudice and hostility exercised against his ethnic group, and therefore, indirectly against himself.

The Negro policeman who accommodates himself in this manner seems to play a crucial role, both in the department and in the Negro community. In the department he tries to bring about a level of cooperation between members of his occupational group who show an unwillingness to cooperate with each other, that is, John Birch policemen and more militant Negro officers. This is done by attempting to cool antagonisms caused by racial disparagements, backbiting, knifing, and misunderstandings, which can only result, if left unchecked, in aggressiveness toward others and the inability to work together. In short, he acts to give the department a semblance of consensus and integration. But he must be careful not to overextend himself in this integrative role, for this may create among his fellow Negro officers surprise, and even intense anger, towards a "Negro" taking the position of a "white." Thus he must be careful not to transgress his personal loyalty to other Negro policemen by trying to be a good public relations man. In the Negro community he may act as a buffer in the true sense of the word between the overzealous white policeman and the intimidating threats, accusations, and verbal abuse of Negroes directed against his brother officer. However, this can be achieved only if the Negro policeman is accepted by *both* his occupational group and the Negro community, which few Negro policemen are.

A third reaction (expressed by only five policemen) was indifference or a positive attitude towards white policemen. For this group the police role acts as a point of reference. None raised any criticism of white policemen per se, nor did any acknowledge contradictions between their expectations of fellow officers and their actual conduct. To the extent that they do perceive contradictions, they either overlook them or are indifferent to them. We would assume that this group gets along with white officers in a community of reciprocal relations. To the extent that this group identifies with the police role, rejecting their identity as Negroes, they cannot be considered threatening to white policemen. It may be indicative that all but one man in this group were police oriented policemen. The following quotations are typical.

> The majority of white police officers are very dedicated to their work and by and large they do a good job. And particularly New York City policemen. I don't think you will find a department, regardless of the individual's personal feelings— New York City police are perhaps more objective in dealing with the public than any other department I know. (24)

> He is just another white policeman. I find it difficult to be impressed by color. I got to a point where I don't consider it whether the guy is white or colored, possibly because there are so many white policemen. (34)

The implication so far is that color, while not relevant as an occupational norm, does in fact intrude upon and influence interpersonal relations. It is a persistent source of strain, tension, and conflict among working policemen. Racial prejudice in social relations, and racial slurs directed against Negro policemen, Negro citizens, and Negro civil rights leaders, are central facts of life to which the Negro policeman must adjust.

However, such prejudice is more than purely psychological, operating as it does at the level of expressed attitudes and opinions. Prejudice is felt to operate at the very level of the operation and organization of the department. All policemen reported widespread discrimination and separation of races on the basis of color, so that Negro policemen are not given opportunities equivalent or similar to those afforded white policemen. Negro policemen feel that not only are white policemen prejudiced and discriminate against them, but that the whole department does as well. They feel this operates at any level: recruitment, assignments to precincts, radio cars, and in rank and divisional assignments.

Only a minority of these policemen felt that discrimination is not overt but subtle and difficult to locate with exactitude. A few of these men also reported no direct personal experience of discrimination, although all of them knew of its having occurred to others, and had heard of it through rumor.

PERCEPTIONS OF DEPARTMENTAL DISCRIMINATION

The unwritten ratio

A typical example of alleged discrimination was in the area of recruitment. A few policemen charged that the standards of qualification for entry into the department were higher for Negroes than for whites. One such allegation was expressed in this way:

> Let's start from the time you take the examination. There is an unwritten ratio right at the beginning. Let's say you pass the written and physical. You're in perfect health, etc. Then comes the character investigation. Take a lot of kids who are locked up for dice—minor things like that—summonses. If you have a previous minor violation you have to tell them. If you don't tell them, and they find out later, your chances of losing your job are very good. When you tell them they give you a court hearing behind this. At that point they can easily stop you from going on. A white guy can have the same minor violation as you but will get in. But they use this minor violation, it's like a gimmick, as a tool to use against you. To keep the ratio of Negroes to white in right perspective. They're not really concerned with the minor violation, but they use it as an excuse and they have this back door meeting to review your background. There are many examples of guys not accepted because of this. The majority of them are Negroes. In addition, you have to show from the time you came out of school how you supported yourself. If you were unemployed you have to show an affidavit from your parents that they kept

care of you. You find yourself sometimes lying about your background to get the job. What else can you do? They pick up everything on you and use it against you. So you lie—even though it's a big chance they can use that lie later on against you. No other way out. On the other hand they are much easier on white policemen regarding this character investigation. (6)

Assignments to precincts

One policeman claimed that when he joined the department (in 1947), Negro officers were usually restricted to Negro precincts. This meant that their patrol and arrest jurisdiction was limited to Negro areas. Consequently, they were excluded from white neighborhoods, he said, and came in contact with few white offenders. Under such circumstances, Negro policemen were not fulfilling the function for which they were presumably hired. They were hired because they were Negroes, and not because they were policemen.

> . . . one time in this department when I came into the job, the Negro policemen were assigned to two or three posts [precincts]. They were assigned to the 79th[2] and the 77th in Brooklyn, and they were assigned to the 28th and the 32nd in Manhattan, and I believe, the 40th precinct. Maybe another precinct. So that the bulk of the Negroes were assigned to these four (excluding the 40th which I'm not sure of). The 77th, a relatively small precinct, was located in a Negro neighborhood two or three blocks away, and on the south side was a white nieighborhood. The 28th and 32nd are right in Harlem. (15)

Another police officer gave a more up-to-date picture of the deployment of Negro policemen to ghetto precincts since the 1940's, and indicated general improvement in this area of assignments.

> Much of the old flagrant discriminatory practices that prevailed prior to the 1940's and to a less degree in the 1950's

[2] The 79th precinct is in Brownsville, a Negro ghetto.

have to a great extent been done away with. It was almost unheard of for a Negro to ride in a radio car—and very few instances, if any, where he received assignments to mixed areas. He was assigned primarily to Negro ghetto areas. Since the time of Commissioner Kennedy, and in fact, slightly preceding his time, in the administration of Commissioner Adams, there has been a manifest integration of the foot patrolman throughout much of the city. (10)

However, he went on to suggest that the department has recently reverted back to the traditional custom of assigning Negro policemen to ghetto precincts, or to neighborhoods with a large Negro population. While the historical justification for keeping Negro policemen in ghetto precincts was based, perhaps, on the fears that Negroes would get uppity if placed in positions of authority over white people, the new policy simply considers it good police tactics to assign Negro patrolmen to ghettoes, because it accommodates a growing vocal demand from Negro citizens, leaders, and civil rights groups for his services in those areas. For instance:

> The integration of the foot patrolman thoughout the city still follows a neighborhood pattern . . . I mean that demands are made for his services by community citizens who feel that the general condition of Harlem could be alleviated by the assignment of more Negro patrolmen there, and of superior officers who had virtually been nonexistent in the area . . . The Guardians Association made an official decision regarding this assignment of Negroes to Harlem . . . They decided that Negro patrolmen were Negroes before they entered the department, and would remain Negroes after they would leave the department . . . We would accept limited transfers of Negro policemen back to Harlem as a scientific police tactic, but we would not lend ourselves to any program that would tend to reverse the ongoing trend toward a complete integration of the department. Some Negro patrolmen were definitely hurt by this decision. They didn't like the assignment, and they don't like the assignment. They had lost good assignments, and are unhappy about the new posts. (10)

106

This assertion is in fact true. Most Negro policemen interviewed were resentful of and angered by the new policy of transferring them to Harlem. The theme that occurs over and over again is that the policy was the result of a "political scheme," which has "ghettoized" the Negro officer, is a "self-imposed form of segregation," and has led to a degree of "isolation" of Negro policemen from work in white precincts. In fact, they had lost good posts in white precincts, posts that were symbolic of their mobility from the lower depths of the ghetto. Moreover, the Negro policeman is assigned to areas on the basis of color, while the police department has no basis in fact for saying that Negroes will be more effective in a Negro community, and, it may be added, where the Negro policeman himself may have no basis to proclaim his effectiveness there. As one policeman commented:

> They strongly objected to being transferred to Harlem for purposes of satisfying a political scheme. If the assignment was due to a natural assignment, it would be all right. But when they were victimized and intentionally put into Harlem, many of them asked why. Oddly enough, historically speaking, when I came into the job, a good proportion of Negro officers went to Negro precincts . . . Since then, many Negro policemen were spread throughout the city . . . Thus many Negro policemen moved from the Harlem area in the sense of bettering themselves and different standards in bringing up children. Now they see themselves back in an area where they don't wish to see themselves assigned . . . No one questioned the Negro police officer to see whether he wanted to go back to Harlem . . . What you really get from all of this is punishment again for being a Negro. (29)

Two policemen considered the transfer a result of "the department backlash." Presumably, the department was punishing the Negro policeman for the gains made by Negro citizens as a result of the civil rights movement.

A few, more realistically, assessed the situation as a response to the legitimate needs of the Negro community for more Negro policemen.

I don't think that this was done to harass the Negro policeman on the part of the department. The area demanded it
because there were more white policemen in the area than
Negro policemen. There have been fewer Negro policemen in
Harlem—they were stretched in the five boroughs. (28)

Yet this statement merely points to the essential paradox confronting the Negro policeman, and has its parallel in what Booker
T. Washington was reported to have said regarding the plight of
the Negro who had advanced to middle-class standing: the Negro
community is like a basket of crabs, wherein should one member
attempt to get out, the others immediately pull him back. This
dilemma, and its consequences for the Negro policeman, is expressed by the following police officer:

We have about 1,450 Negro policemen. Most of the major
civil rights groups would like to see more Negro policemen
in Harlem. This is good and bad. What do you call it, self-
imposed segregation? I say if they flood a Harlem area with
all Negro policemen, that in itself limits policemen in other
areas to work in. (2)

Assignments to radio cars

There is a general agreement among Negro policemen that they
are for the most part denied radio car patrol duty. One policeman
gave the criteria which should be used in assigning men to this
desirable duty, then concluded from his own observations and
experiences that these criteria are not applied in the case of Negro
patrolmen.

There are two ways to determine who shall ride in a car on a
regular basis. One is based on the man's activity (arrests,
etc.). Another is based on his seniority. And a third, a com-
bination of the two. At my house [precinct] there are men who
haven't been there a year and they are riding which means
it is not based on seniority. Again, I know Negro officers

who hold the highest arrest record and general activity and they don't ride. (39)

One policeman commented on the consequences of not riding in patrol cars.

> They say that 90 percent of the work is done by people in radio motor cars, and you will find very few Negro policemen in radio cars. And the policeman in the radio car does 90 percent of the patrol work. That is, he will be coming into contact with people in need of assistance more frequently than the man on post. But the Negro policeman is kept away from this and consequently kept away from the contact with people and the work. (27)

When he is assigned this duty, it is more than likely that he will be assigned to a Negro sector.

> Very often you would find Negro policemen who had worked in only the slum portion of the precinct. If assigned to a radio car he would get the sector where the population consisted of Puerto Ricans and Negroes. (23)

Rank and divisional assignments

Two other sources of potential discrimination against Negro policemen are those regarding the areas of divisional assignments (for instance, the detective division), specialized units or squads (such as the homicide squad), and the areas of rank. One policeman referred to some of the specialized units and divisions which do not have Negroes. In addition, he offered some reasons for this.

> Very prevalent. The system of the job created it. Negroes were about the last to come into the job. There is definitely a caste system in the department. The caste system excludes Negroes in many areas. He didn't associate with white offi-

109

cers and consequently wasn't considered for any good positions in the hierarchy. One reason for being excluded in the police department was because society and its system excluded him from certain places. There are many areas within the department which exclude Negroes—he doesn't belong in these areas. The Negro couldn't function in the Confidential Squad which try to infiltrate certain groups because the Confidential Squad is all white, or least most of the investigators are white. Other places where the Negro can't enter: The Safe and Loft Squad, the Burglary Squad (most of these are detectives), certain divisions of the Fraud Squad, and in certain detective precincts where there are no Negro detectives. (14)

The following policemen pointed to other specialized units and jobs that do not have Negroes.

Have a Homicide Squad in Manhattan North where 80 percent of the homicides are Negro. They don't have any Negroes assigned! They had one who asked out because of the treatment he received. There was one fellow who insisted on going there but he never got in. So he got disgusted and so he went sick on an old injury. He forced the issue where they either had to put him in or drop him and they found a reason not to accept him. So he played sick on this old injury. And he now has a nothing detail. (33)

. . . the T.S. assignment (telephone switchboard) and Negroes are not assigned to this. Then there is the turnkey attendant. Not one station to my knowledge has one Negro attendant. (39)

A superior officer had this to say regarding discrimination in specalized units.

At headquarters you have an office of Community Relations. There are twenty-five people in it. And only recently, since the riots last summer [1964], did they put a Negro in this office. All these years they did not have one Negro policeman

110

in this office. Actually the name is a misnomer, but they were stuck with the name. Actually, it was a public relations outfit, but even a public relations outfit should have some representation. (21)

Apparently affirming these remarks, and indicating the difficulty experienced by Negroes trying to enter the detective division, one policeman said:

> If you are the boss you can keep anyone out. The Irish are the bosses. It's an Irish job and they want to keep it. They can't stop you on the promotion jobs, because you take a test and the marks are posted, so everyone knows. But they can stop you from getting into the Detectives, Youth Division, and Plainclothes. (8)

Discrimination is also believed to exist in the areas of rank above captain. As one police officer remarked:

> You don't have enough Negroes for the sergeant's position— that is, you don't have enough Negro men applying for the position. The list is posted and whites and Negroes are studying for the examination, and consequently, not many Negroes are in this position. On the other hand, advancement above the rank of captain—it's all political and strings. It's only my opinion, but there are no Negro inspectors whatsoever. The reasons for that is because of politics—you have politicians who control all that—consequently there must be discrimination for positions which are not filled by examination. (5)

The structure of police organization does in fact allow discrimination to take place in the areas of rank. For example, while men enter the police department by way of civil service examination, and are promoted by examinations, advancement under civil service rules and regulations stops at the rank of captain, making it the highest "permanent" rank in the force. All ranks above captain are subject to the Police Commissioner's power of "discretion and direction" in appointing men to fill these positions. This

111

power of appointment also applies to the detective division, including advancement within the agency, as well as the assignment of policemen to specific precincts, squads, or any other specialized branch of police service.[3]

Thus, there is a considerable amount of discretion built into the police structure allowing discrimination to take place on the basis of color or other criteria. Although it is difficult to say that a man has not been promoted to a given rank either by civil service examination or appointment or to a particular specialized unit or squad because he is a Negro, many Negro officers believe that such discretion has been used as a means of racial discrimination.

What is the solution to the status contradictions confronting the Negro policeman? It might lie in creating conditions under which it is no longer important and no longer gainful to stigmatize the Negro because of his color. As one policeman reminds us:

> The Negro police officer has been a product of a system that has historically relegated certain groups to second-class citizenship; a system fostered and perpetuated by municipal, state, and federal laws, church practices, and as a result, by the very mores—not to forget the utter distortion of United States history, distorted by design. He is not only in the middle of this, he is willingly or knowingly, actually an integral part of what all minority groups find anti. Only when the police hierarchy by action comes to grips with this basic truth and adopts a police policy to conform therewith, and only then, will we see a beginning or a resolution to the problem. (10)

The comments in this chapter reveal something of what happens to Negroes who have achieved occupational mobility. We have seen that even when the Negro acquires the advantages that limited opportunities had historically precluded for him, he is still far from achieving the full status that the job implies for his white counterpart. The recognition of the Negro policeman primarily

[3] Ibid., pp. 47-51. This was substantiated by the Negro policemen in our study.

112

as a Negro is reinforced by the behavior of white colleagues, and by an internal occupational stratification through which he is assigned, once again, second-class citizenship. Yet as will be seen in the next chapter, even when he acquires good posts in white precincts, his race continues to act as a barrier, separating him from his official status.

— 5

The white public

We have seen that the Negro policeman's subordinate position within the department contributes to his insecurity as a man. It is equally clear that this insecurity is sustained by the fact that he often does not receive assurance from his white counterparts that he is a policeman. But this is also true in his dealings with the white public. His failure to register in his official role with white clientele accounts for further problems of status dilemmas.

While his importance in the Negro community may derive from the fact that he is above all else a policeman, his importance in dealing with the white public derives from the fact that he is essentially a Negro. While he has authority by virtue of his institutional position, he is more likely treated on unequal terms because of his racial origin. In this sense he is a representative of two forces, from which it follows that the authority given him as a public servant and society's designation of him as inferior are incongruent.

To take on an authority-vested role has inevitably resulted in a measure of alienation from his own subculture and ethnic group status. In some cases while accepting the identity of a Negro, he has deprecated the contents of that identity as expressed by the deprived life styles of the Negro ghetto. Yet, paradoxically, his mobility as a policeman, and his opportunity to carry out an official service for whites, has prevented him from completely realizing his police role in its fullest sense. In the eyes of the white public he is sometimes seen as inadequate for the job simply because he is black. The white feels uneasy about him—he is, after all, a member of a minority exercising authority—which in turn makes him uneasy. Any situation he meets is potentially able to reveal something different from what he expects. Thus the problem of the Negro policeman is not only finding a role, but discovering that any role, any identity, he may choose can change into another role, another identity, almost without warning.

A NEWCOMER

This view—that one is not completely accepted in the role of police officer—was voiced by the following policeman's reply to the question, "What are some of the attitudes of white citizens towards the Negro police officer?"

> From a personal point of view I don't feel as comfortable as I would in a Negro neighborhood. (40)

When asked why he felt uncomfortable, he continued:

> You may feel right from the start that the inhabitants may be more critical of you because of maybe their first contacts with you . . . it is like the feeling of a Negro being seen when he has never been seen before. You can sense when you get extra observation. By being critical I mean that the whites are more awed and more eager to see what my actions would be,

what actions I would take. They want to evaluate you and see what type of protection they are going to get. (40)

Such an answer implies that he is viewed as a newcomer to the police role. In this connection, they are curious about him because of his color, and uneasy toward him because they question his role as police officer—in effect, as this policeman indicates, what action he will take. Will it be as a Negro policeman or as a policeman? Another policeman's answer was similar:

I feel if he works a steady post where people see him every day and get to know him, there are no problems. But white people are not accustomed to seeing a Negro as a policeman. And because of that, the white person will have reservations about the Negro policeman. You get the stares, for example, from people who are not accustomed to seeing you. They look at him as a Negro policeman and not as a policeman. (27)

However, another officer expressed the feeling that it was not because he was a Negro that the curiosity of whites was aroused, but simply because he was a "new police officer." Color was inconsequential. But this isolated case was not the majority view.

When I started out in the police department I had been told this in police school and it was a fact that I was a new police officer not a Negro police officer. And people seem to have a tendency to be repelled by a new police officer because they don't know you. They look at you curiously. What are you going to do? What are you not going to do? You get all kinds of reactions. But, not knowing you is the main thing here. (31)

Contrary to this response, the newcomer role based on color was supported by a substantial majority of replies to the question, "Do you find it harder or easier than a white policeman working in a white neighborhood?" This comment was typical.

Yes, I think it is harder for a Negro officer in a white neighborhood. It is harder for a Negro policeman working any-

117

where! It is harder because people don't understand you. I think that white people are not willing to accept the Negro policeman because they associate him with the Harlem area. I think they feel that the Negro police officer does not have the intelligence of the situation the way they feel it should be coped with. This I can speak for personally. Quite often they treat him as a Negro rather than as a police officer . . . They just can't believe that a Negro can be a policeman. (12)

The newcomer role sometimes takes the form of public resentment towards the Negro who is a policeman. And this resentment can be seen as a form of resolution to the dilemma confronting his white clientele, namely, whether they will respond to him as a policeman or as a Negro. To the extent that he is perceived as a member of an inferior social category, he might be identified as one who has usurped the status of police officer. That is, the white public may feel his status as a policeman should not have been or could not have been earned in a functionally and socially useful way simply because of their stereotyped view of him. This resentment was expressed in the following typical experiences:

> Every once in a while, you would find a situation when a person would refuse to give you his license, or he would throw the license down on the ground for you to pick up when you stopped him for speeding or something like that, and he was white. Or a person would tell me if I didn't have a shield or gun, what would I do? (30)

> White people might say to me: Why don't you arrest some niggers. I want to be arrested by a white man. (34)

One policeman told how he accommodates himself to the dilemma of his status contradictions, as evoked by similar provocations.

> The Negro officer knows he has to put forth much more than a white officer. He has to be particularly sharp, to raise himself above the suspicions and doubts that citizens have towards him. In my experience it is true—I felt it as a challenge

> to cope with a situation—where you enter an apartment and the person seemed to be shocked that you are a Negro officer. This is the challenge—to see their faces—and to show them that I can handle my job as well as another police officer, and leave them with a feeling that I have done a good job. I don't think there is anything more gratifying to a police officer than to have a person compliment him and commend him on the way he has handled a situation. (12)

Incomplete acceptance as a police officer does not in fact stop him from attempting to transcend his status as a Negro. Consequently even though he faces social situations which are consistently contrary to what he expects in his official role, he has not given up. He still feels that he has a chance to be accepted in this role. In fact, the contradictory situations he finds reinforce identification with his professional role.

Another policeman offered the following form of adaptation to similar problems he faces with the white public.

> Mostly, you are aware of the fact that you are a Negro—a Negro policeman. So you have to be aware of what you do is strictly by the book. You don't have the convenience of being a cop but a Negro cop. I was in a precinct where there were 200 cops and I was the only Negro. Some civilian might say a Negro cop did that to me. If this gets back to any guy in the precinct, he knows who it is—me. I don't have the privilege of being anonymous as a policeman. But if a civilian says some white cop did this to me, well, it's a different story. He is just a cop and there are 200 of them in the precinct. (34)

Because of his visibility, and because of the small number of Negro policemen in the department (especially those who work in white neighborhoods), he is easily spotted. Any transgression can be easily traced to its source. He must control himself carefully. Since he is a Negro, the social situation he confronts demands strict conformity to his police role, as defined by police regulations.

Both of the above policemen, then, perceive themselves as new to the role, and consequently are given a careful scrutiny by the white public. After all, they *are* Negroes; can they then still be loyal to the needs and interests of the white community?

The newcomer role shows the Negro policeman that the white community essentially distrusts him. It also serves to remind him, more often than not, that he is excluded from being considered a policeman. But above and beyond the boundaries separating him from the community in which he works is the interior problem of what he feels he can do and is, and what his experiences tell him. Thus there are limits between his official role and the clientele that he should serve, and the gap between his own sense of position and the actual role that he plays.

However, it is the attempt to cross both exterior and interior limits that defines the character of the Negro civil servant. He attempts to cross the limits by asserting himself in his official role. But the more he asserts himself in his relations with white citizens, the more they may feel he is acting "too much the cop because he wants to get even on the whole race issue." Again, the Negro policeman is caught by the conditions of his dual positions. For example:

> Do you remember the incident when Emett Till was killed? A white motorist was angry at me because I gave him a ticket and said I was giving him a ticket because of what had happened to Emett Till around that time. I couldn't even remember who Till was. Another illustration: I had a Negro woman who I asked to move her car from where it was double parked and she told me if she was white I wouldn't have asked her to move. (17)

Thus, in conforming to the police role in the hope, perhaps, of becoming an established member of the police, the Negro officer may not be given this opportunity when his actions as a policeman are interpreted as consequences of his race. The result is ambivalent in the sense that, because of his color, he is necessarily defined in terms of something else. He can only hope to become an insider by strict adherence to his professional role, although this conformity will only confirm his role as a partial outsider. Furthermore, to the extent that he works in white areas and

120

claims deference to an occupational status that is not granted to him, his ethnic group peers may judge the relation as conspiratorial and characterize this type of conformity as accepting the authority of the ruling group. There is, though, the possibility that he may accept his identity as a Negro, but consider himself an exception.

The Negro policeman has the same official authority, power, and legal status as that of the white policeman. However, he feels that there are limitations in the exercise of this power and authority when working in white areas, or when arresting white wrong-doers—and these limitations are rooted in his feeling that because he is a Negro, this fact makes his police authority ambiguous. The following perceptive comment indicates that the Negro policeman may not be as assertive as a white policeman in his relations with whites because of a racial psychology of powerlessness.

> No, a Negro policeman would not have it harder working in a white neighborhood. The Negro policeman would be conscious of the fact that he is in a white area, and because he has never had the advantage of being in power, he would not make any attempt to take advantage—police action—unless he was reasonably sure. A Negro in a white community, realizing he is in a white community, would have to be pretty sure of action he would take because he wouldn't feel secure or on safe ground. He also would realize that anything he did do would be brought to the attention of the department. He would definitely feel less powerful in a white neighborhood because even though he is a policeman with certain vested powers, he still would feel less powerful, or, no better than his exposure to whites in regular Negro-white relationships. In regular relationships he is in a powerless position. In a uniform, he is still in a powerless position regarding whites.
>
> I will give you an example of this: I went into an Italian restaurant some time ago with a group of white fellows. I was the only Negro with the group and the only Negro in the restaurant. Well, I can assure you that I didn't feel too comfortable in that restaurant even though nothing was said to me by anyone sitting there. But the feeling of being very uncomfortable was definitely there. Now because of the fact

that the two races live apart and that their fusing them doesn't happen until they have reached the high school age, there is a lack of communication. And also, realizing the fact that the attitudes of the parents of the child of what they can do and can't do (knowing that they are placed in a powerless position regarding rights, and what is allowed by his parents early in life), these things influence his attitudes to the white community. So, even though the Negro policeman is vested with powers, he still may be influenced by an attitude instilled in him by his parents from the time he was a child in his relationship to whites. The uniform is only a surface kind of power. His basic attitudes have been set up regarding Negro-white relationships. And I think this is the reason that he is very sure before he acts in such a community. Because his history is that of bondage and this is not changed by the wearing of the uniform. (29)

The Negro's low self-esteem is in no way alleviated by his authority role. His "psychology of oppression" may cause him to be less confident and assertive in his relations with "influential" white citizens. But caution in the exercise of his duty may have the effect of destroying his self-respect as a professional policeman, as well as the respect that others have of him. For the professional policeman is obligated to make an arrest wherever and whenever an arrest is required. Yet the Negro policeman who does *in fact* assert himself in his official role may also be in trouble, as indicated by the following policeman who took "liberties" by arresting a middle-class white youth who committed a misdemeanor. Although arresting a white wrongdoer may be the only unambiguous situation that the Negro policeman confronts, and he may find some satisfaction in asserting his authority in such situations, the costs to him may be great.

> I arrested some kid driving 90 miles an hour in a 35 mile an hour zone. He was a white kid and I stopped him in Richmond Hill. I asked him for his license and he wouldn't give it to me. I said: You're under arrest. I put him in a cab, and we went to the precinct. In the precinct he threw a punch at me and connected. I gave him a smack with my hand that hurt

him, and he started to cry. I am sure he was never hit that way. As I brought the kid up to the sergeant's desk, the sergeant tells me: Hey, ———, what in the hell are you doing? Do you know who this kid is? I said, I don't care who he is or what his father is—his father was a lawyer. They called the captain down from his house. He put pressure on me not to make the arrest. I told the captain that as an officer I made the observation that this kid had broken the law and that he (his father) was in bed at the time and wouldn't know what had happened, and he wasn't in the position to say. Also, the kid's father came and talked and talked. I said: It seems that there is a lot of talk, but nobody seems to want to hear what happened. This kid could have killed somebody. I think if I was his father, I would tell him something. The lawyer was mad and said to me that I was lecturing him! I said I wasn't lecturing him but only stating an opinion about his son and what I would do if I was his father. To make a long story short, this was the beginning of a number of transfers I made within the department. Matter of fact, this incident led me to ——— Park. I became a park cop. This is regarded within the department as the end of the line. You are sent there for being an oddball or a troublemaker. Anyhow, this was the last incident that led to the ——— Park detail. There is absolutely nothing to do there. You read the papers, study for promotional examinations . . . (14)

Certainly one's social adjustment to the situation is important here. However, it would seem that the subservient position the Negro police officer occupies because of his color is a social force defining much of what can be said regarding the form of police action he is allowed to take in white areas, institutional authority to the contrary. A fundamental problem facing the Negro policeman in white neighborhoods (as well as in the Negro community) is how to maintain his position and integrity as a policeman while adjusting to the role definitions made by his clientele.

Further confirmation of the powerless position he occupies *de facto* was given by another police officer. Although he had never worked in a white neighborhood, he anticipated a situation that could confront him.

I haven't worked in a white precinct, so I wouldn't know
about this. I know that I would not feel at ease as I do now in
a Negro precinct and Negro neighborhood. It seems that I
think that a Negro cop stands out. He stands out because he
is a Negro in a white background. Any actions that he takes
by himself, is taken on by the white citizens, and tends to
make the cop nervous. He is nervous because he is under observation. On one night, around Fulton Street where I was
working, this fellow was kicking this girl under the car. I
subdued him and walked him to the corner of Nostrand and
Fulton, a well-known corner and very active. I tried to get this
guy to put his hands up while I searched him. He was a
Negro. When he didn't comply, I hit him with a stick on the
forehead, causing a small cut on his eyebrow. To my surprise,
the local citizens, the Negro citizens, said good. That is what
these young punks need. Now, why am I saying this? Well, I
don't think I would be able to hit someone with a stick in a
white neighborhood as I did to this Negro in a Negro neighborhood. I don't think the reaction of citizens would have
been the same. What would they have seen? I think they
would have seen a Negro hitting a white person, not a Negro
cop hitting a rowdy. They would be more apt to accept it if a
white cop hit a white person. (7)

The following policeman who has worked in white precincts
directs our attention to similar kinds of problems. The Negro
policeman is viewed by whites as just a Negro who has no "connections."

Whites feel that because you are a Negro, you don't have any
connections. The white person is assured of this. And the
white person is also assured that the Negro cop, because he is
Negro, is limited in scope and in attitude to alleviate their
particular problem. (19)

One policeman offered the paradoxical view that whites do not
respond to his official authority, but respond to the fact that he is
a stranger to the community, a newcomer. They respond to the
novelty and newness of seeing a Negro in uniform having arrest

jurisdiction over whites. However, he also indicated that because he is a Negro, new to the police role, the white public may not respond to his police status thus forcing him to overreact.

> When I worked in an all white neighborhood, I never had any trouble. I think the Negro community, however, will accept the white person more readily than the white community is accepting the Negro.
> I worked for six months in an all white area with another Negro cop. You tell citizens to move, they move. You tell him to put that coin in the meter, he runs over there and he does it. Why? Because they don't know you. You are a novelty. You stand out. This standing out, and you being strange, make them move. Many white people, if you tell them to move, and if they don't—you assert yourself. I'm also a policeman you try and tell them. If you don't respect me for what I am then respect my uniform. (4)

At times the Negro policeman may be given the respect to which he feels his uniform entitles him, and it is granted because he is a representative of the white public, performing a service for which it pays. As a policeman, he is the white community's public servant, in the true sense of the word. When the white public shows deference to him, it does so because he carries out functions which are required and needed by whites. For instance:

> The white citizens respond to him as an officer. They respond to him this way because they feel that they have power over the Negro cop. If you hit a civilian the wrong way, he makes a few telephone calls. But they respect you as an officer. (14)

The respect afforded him implies that he has accepted the authority of the white public. After all, he is the guardian of white society. He can only remain a police officer as long as he conforms to the role of public servant. Another policeman acknowledged this:

> I work in a white neighborhood. They treat me as an equal. I protect them. They treat me like a human being. I help their

125

kids across the street. But I don't know what their opinions are of me. But they treat me square. (23)

However, the public servant role signifies other meanings to the Negro policeman as well. For example:

> I worked in a white neighborhood for seven years. And when I first came over there, there was like a feeling-you-out thing. Lot of people talked down to you. And in that neighborhood, there is a lot of domestic help and doormen. And I think most of the relations between the white people and the Negro people was on the basis of an employer-employee basis. One night I had a white lady come up to me—I was in uniform—to call her a cab. I politely ignored her request. You get little antennas out as a Negro, and you can tell when a person is being hostile to you. (17)

> Whenever you work in the city—work in Park Avenue or lower Park Avenue—where you work with the affluent, these people have no respect for the uniform. To them, you are a servant. You are there to cater to what they want. With the affluent group, they feel superior to you. To them you are like a doorman. (12)

White policemen may feel the same way. This would be especially true if they were asked to perform a service (such as calling a cab for a lady) obviously beyond the call of police duty, even in those instances where gratuities may be expectedly forthcoming. But such requests are interpreted, at least implied, by Negro policemen as having racial overtones, and are not associated with the Negro policeman's proper status and character. While he may not know what his status is, or at least not be aware of its ambiguity, he does know that these requests are insulting and demeaning to him. Often, nothing he can say or do in his official role will make the slightest difference to the outcome of being defined by race. Thus when whites insist on defining him in terms of his color (that is, where the Negro policeman picks up racial cues and clues), the rest is simply association and suggestion of being included in the category of a Negro or Puerto Rican

126

doorman, or even a uniformed Negro domestic. The history of using uniformed Negroes to perform menial labor for the pleasure and comfort of whites is not inconsistent with this view. In fact, the vested meaning of the Negro in uniform merely confirms the role of relationships of "superior white" and "inferior Negro." The police role in this sense incorporates in its image all that can be said regarding the public "servant" role. That whites may feel the Negro policeman is something different from what he expects may be beside the point. They simply give him the identity they can use best, by calling upon him to perform menial services which they consider to be in accord with his racial "inferiority."

Therefore, while he may consider himself as having uplifted his class position through occupational mobility, and make claims to the prestige benefits implied in this position, the fact of racial identity and association makes this class distinction ambiguous, if not impossible. For the only way a Negro policeman could be accepted as an officer without reference to color would be in a thoroughly integrated society. Only where it is impossible to identify the members of the group to which a racial stigma is attached can the Negro policeman hope to be identified simply as a policeman. Such a condition is unlikely to be fulfilled in the present state of the community.

But there are some qualifications to this. Namely, a few Negro policemen expressed an appreciation of the socioeconomic class groupings of whites. In broadest outline, this group of officers felt their problems in white areas were not so much a consequence of race differences but a function of class. The higher the socioeconomic status of the white, the greater the likelihood that he will respond to the Negro as a policeman, and give him the respect he feels he is entitled to. One officer introduced this hypothesis:

> It depends on the type of neighborhood and the class of people in it. If you take downtown (mid-Manhattan) people are much more pleasant. The white people tend to have much more respect for the Negro cop than Negroes have for the Negro cop. But I think it depends more on class than color. The middle-class people will give you less trouble than

the lower-class people every time. Any cop, regardless of his color, who works in a middle-class neighborhood will have a better time of it. (8)

As shall be seen, this comment is supported by the Negro policemen's experiences in Negro areas. Negro policemen are given more respect by middle-class Negroes than by lower-class Negroes, and in turn, have an easier time adjusting to their police role.

There is no consistency, however, among these policemen who offer class as a factor in evaluating the problems they confront and the way in which they are seen by their clientele. One policeman, for example, suggests that it is more difficult to adjust and that there are generally greater problems for him in such a neighborhood. In effect he implies that the higher the status of the whites, the greater the tendency for the white person to differentiate between high and low status occupations held by Negroes. For example, he stated:

> . . . There is a general rule that in an all white community you have a higher socioeconomic group than in an area which is mixed. Anytime this is true the policeman's job becomes more difficult whether he is white or whether he is Negro. For one thing, for the average police officer it is more difficult for him to relate to a teacher, doctor, or lawyer than to relate to a longshoreman. The police officer would be more apprehensive on his part as to whether he is doing the right thing or not. He feels that the guy with the higher status can articulate his grievance better. It is also the fact that the higher status person has friends who can come to his aid. This is one of the big issues the civil rights groups have made. A police officer on Park Avenue wouldn't even speak to a person going through a red light as he would if the person going through a red light was a Negro. (24)

By introducing national origin as a variant in the problems confronted by Negro officers, another policeman added to the hesitation we might have in making any generalizations on the basis of class.

128

If the Negro cop were in an Irish, German, or Italian neighborhood, then, they would be hard on him. If he worked in a Jewish neighborhood, they wouldn't be hard on him. The neighborhood I worked in was 85 percent Jewish. I've worked in other neighborhoods (non-Jewish) and I don't like working there. As a matter of fact, in my neighborhood, the SPONGE group [Society to Prevent Negroes from Getting Everything] originated there. They are still there. When I read that article (an article that appeared in the newspapers regarding this group and their harassment of CORE members at the World's Fair), I shivered. I hoped the people in the neighborhood didn't read the article. The neighborhood is definitely anti-Negro. If the information gets out there will definitely be trouble. The guy who organized the club is psycho and Italian. (15)

Another policeman offered a contradictory picture.

The only white neighborhood that I worked in was predominantly a Jewish neighborhood. And the Jewish people by and large tend to blow up [at] minor things, such as: three boys were singing rock and roll down the street, and a woman comes out and says that this is disturbing the peace . . . They are also suspicious of me as a Negro. I had a situation where I had a call for a burglary. In this case two men hit the building. Both go into the building. One guy stands by the door in the building, and the other guy goes up the fire escape to box him in. I knocked on the door and the woman is looking at me through the peep hole. I'm in uniform and I'm trying to explain to her what I wanted. She becomes petrified, and she assumed me of being a robber, that I was going to rape her, and that I was using this as an excuse to get into her apartment even though I had the uniform on. Another incident along these lines. Got a call one afternoon that a man was exposing himself. A man I had originally asked if he knew anything about the call denied it to me. The sergeant, who is white, goes to the same guy and gets the information. He tells the sergeant about the call. The man who was exposing himself was a man who was working in the garden and didn't have his shirt on. That was the nature of the exposure. The man that was stripped was a Negro. (32)

In short, the socioeconomic class of the neighborhood, presumably an important variable affecting the interpersonal patterns and adjustments of Negro officer–white clientele, is not in fact supported by our data.

Be it noted in passing that sex is a potential focal point (and taboo area) for Negro officer-white relations. These policemen strongly implied that sex is unavoidably present in defining the attitudes with which white clientele and Negro policemen regard each other. To the extent that a Negro policeman violates this taboo area, there will be repercussions for him. Sex, in this sense, is intimately associated with the individual's racial role. For example:

> There was one fellow I arrested on a complaint of his girl friend. He wasn't Negro—they were a mixed couple. And he sued the city, false arrest, etc. He said I beat him up, and he said that the reason that I beat him up was that he was going with a Negro woman. But she arrested him, I didn't. And I was accompanied by two white officers at the time. (36)

Another officer talked about the problems he meets when coming to the aid of a white woman.

> A woman was pregnant. The husband meets you at the door. Wife is ready to have a baby. You call the ambulance. Hasn't arrived yet. Time is getting short. You say: Let me see your wife. He says: You want to see my wife? You say: Lady, did your water break? The man looks at you and says: Look, I don't want you talking to my wife that way—I don't even want you looking at my wife. Why in the hell do they send people like you here anyhow? He tells the sergeant that he doesn't want me to look at his wife. The sergeant tells him that I am a police officer. It goes on like that. (30)

This policeman went on to remark about similar problems that are created for him while working with his white counterpart.

> Another time, a white cop asks me whether I got any white women in this precinct. And I told him that if I did I wouldn't tell him about it! Another time a white cop asks me about getting him some colored girls on Fulton Street. I told him sure if you get me some girls from Flatbush. He never spoke to me since. (30)

Such experiences suggest that perhaps sex is an area in which the Negro policeman is made to feel his "inferiority." No doubt it is also realized that the Negro policeman in his confrontation with white females must be careful not to violate the special etiquette of racial relations in today's society.

In conclusion, all of the traditional limitations in Negro-white relations, in the areas of sex, women, etiquette, deference, power, authority, and social status, are superimposed on the white-Negro policeman relations. The problem of the Negro policeman is the white and his stereotypes.

6

The Negro community

The Negro, more than perhaps a member of any other group, is bound by his ethnic definition even when he becomes a policeman. We have indicated that the white public treats him as a Negro more than as a policeman, and that white policemen place him in the special role of being a *Negro* policeman. This is also true of the Negro community since the policeman is an anathema to large segments of the Negro community. The Negro ceases to be a Negro when he becomes a policeman. He becomes an agent for the white society and is reminded of his special class status as a Negro by those in the Negro community with whom he deals.

The term community is not used here in the standard definition of territorial community, or geographic locality, within which

133

all the activities of the individual can be carried out,[1] but rather in the sense of a psychological identity or psychological community where geographic boundaries are not relevant.[2] But given the vast cleavages within the ghetto in which there is relatively little goal consensus, a relatively small amount of participation, vast amounts of apathy, personal retreat, and withdrawal, one can hardly maintain that a genuine community exists.

At most the Negro ghetto implies that there are quasi- (*de-facto*) spatial boundaries within which a Negro can live and be regarded by himself and outsiders as a normal part of the environment. Yet in the following reactions we will refer to the concept of the Negro community because in some of its consequences the Negro masses taken collectively are viewed as a significant factor in social events.

From a political point of view white politicians conceive of Negro voters as being able to influence local, state, and at times, national elections. Therefore they treat Negroes as a functioning community. In practice, however, this means that the Negro community consists of articulate Negro leaders and groups in, say, Brooklyn and Harlem who can influence the voting of Negroes in elections. There are Negro political leaders in the Democratic Party who must be gratified minimally to ensure the delivery of their votes. Thus, Negroes as a voting block, regardless of their various leadership groups, can still be regarded as a community. In addition, Negroes as potential rioters and disturbers of the peace can force white leaders and lawmakers to regard them as a significant and influential pressure group.

From the standpoint of the policeman, the concept of the Negro community does not include all of the Negroes in a specific ghetto. It only means those organized and unorganized groups, real and imaginary (that is, reference groups) which impinge upon him. It may include his family, friends, peers, neighbors,

[1] This definition of community is reflected in the work of Robert M. MacIver and Charles H. Page, *Society: An Introductory Analysis* (New York, Rinehart, 1955), pp. 281-284.

[2] For a conception of the community that emphasizes the psychological dimension see Joseph Bensman, *Status Communities in an Urban Society: The Musical Community*, unpublished, especially pp. 5-8.

and social and civil rights groups to which he belongs, or which are able to impress their views upon him, or whose views he has accepted.

The "community" may not be organized, unified, or operative as an entity; nevertheless parts of it will bring pressure to bear on both the individual policemen and white leaders. The community, then, will be a reference point for those who deal with the Negro, even though its meaning will differ for each person and from issue to issue.

This chapter deals with the specific subgroups within the community which present special opportunities and difficulties for the Negro policeman, and with the techniques he develops to secure and maintain his authority as a policeman in the face of diverse challenges. Some of the problems that arise in his role as neighbor will be considered first.

FRIENDS AND NEIGHBORS

The majority of Negro policemen in this study reside in segregated urban districts that are populated largely or entirely by Negroes. Most also work in the neighborhood or surrounding area in which they reside, or in ghetto areas where they once lived. They do not enjoy the luxury of their white counterparts who may work in Negro territory, but after their tour of duty can go home to their "lily white" communities. The Negro policeman is constantly confronted as a policeman, and always reminded of his Negro identity, even when he is not on the job in his official capacity. He cannot have the comfort during his off-duty hours of concealing his identity as a policeman, try as he may. A departmental ruling requiring police officers to wear their uniforms to and from work has not allowed him this indulgence. He is always a policeman to his friends and neighbors whether he likes it or not. This means that he is bound by the stereotype of the cop— which is an attempt to define the role of the uniform itself in society—regardless of the man who wears it. The stereotype—at times a caricature—is an attempt by Negro citizens to personify

135

the oppressive force of society as evinced by police methods. Thus while the Negro policeman shares with other Negroes a community of *place*, there is not a community of *interest*. The fact that he is a cop, and a Negro one at that, necessarily works against a sense of identification or psychological community. In these terms, his work cannot be a basis for a mutal accommodation of interests, for he is viewed as an alien white influence. The Negro policeman is therefore isolated from the community in which he lives. It must also be realized that the Negro policeman, coming from the lower and lower middle class, shares some of these same attitudes towards the police. And his experiences as a policeman has not proved otherwise. To the extent that he is alienated from the community he is alienated from himself. He may overcome some of this alienation by seeking identification with his occupational community. But, as has been shown, he is not permitted to do this because of the attitude of the white policemen. The attempt to find a community that embraces race and occupation has resulted in the Guardians, a line organization of black policemen.

One policeman introduces some of the foregoing problems in describing his off-duty hours.

> There is no doubt that the white officer has a rough time in a Negro neighborhood. On the other hand, with a white officer, after he finishes his 8-hour tour of duty, he can go home and forget what he has done—maybe what *damage* he has done. The Negro police officer quite often is stymied along these lines because predominantly he is living in a Negro neighborhood. Because of this fact, he will get the same problems twenty-four hours a day. The Negro officer will get complaints from Negro citizens of what a white officer has done to so-and-so. You can either shrug your shoulders and walk away—you can try and appease them and tell them that this particular officer was only trying to do his duty. You can try to sympathize with them. When you do this, this doesn't satisfy them as far as their animosity toward the white police officer is concerned, but makes you more friendly toward your own kind. But it is a situation of living with your own kind too—and you can't say it was this white officer's fault.

136

> Because if you say that he was at fault in a particular situa-
> tion, what you do is help reinforce their hostile feelings to-
> ward you as a police officer. The more you take their position
> regarding the situation—that is, the more you side with
> them, the more hostile they became toward the cop—and you
> happen to be a cop, and indirectly, you give them fuel to
> hate you. (12)

This double bind situation was seen from different aspects by
the same policeman. He feels that it is especially difficult for the
Negro policeman who lives and works in Harlem.

> I know several police officers who live in Harlem. They grew
> up there and many of the people they arrest are people they
> grew up with. One of my best friends while I was going to
> high school is a junky today. I see him very often but he will
> not speak to me. He won't speak to me because of what I am,
> and because of where he is today. He told another friend of
> mine that he would never speak to me because of that. This
> is a sad commentary. Now as far as I am concerned, I don't
> know how I will react if I saw him do something wrong. The
> possibility of catching him either in the act of stealing, or
> possessing narcotics is very good. But I don't know what I
> would do. This puts me in a bind. I would have to make a
> decision to go one way or the other when we do meet in such
> a situation. What way I would go—I don't really know. (12)

A possible solution to the ambiguities, tensions, and questions
to which this policeman poignantly refers, is not to be recognized
as a policeman. However, the typical replies to the question, "Do
your neighbors know you are a policeman?" indicate the ever-
recurrent theme among the forty-one policemen who were asked
to comment: they know, and it is bad that they know.

> As of last summer the regulations were changed to make us
> wear our uniform to and from work.[3] So now they all know.
> It's not now a matter of first being Jimmy. This is out
> now. Now there are always police problems that come up

[3] This regulation has since been rescinded.

after duty. There is always conversation along police lines. Where we used to talk about baseball or football, it's now talk about police work. They don't let me forget who I am. In this neighborhood I thought I would be better off because so many cops live in the neighborhood. And I figured people would be used to having a cop as a neighbor and accept you as a neighbor. In my old neighborhood where I was making about twice the salary anybody else was making they attached a status symbol to the job. My new neighborhood, where there are a lot of cops and professionals, I thought would be different in atmosphere than it is. (32)

The above responses strongly indicate that in a Negro neighborhood friends easily become enemies and neighbors don't let policemen forget their position. This suggests the power of neighbors to define the policeman's role and to respond to him exclusively in these terms. Also, Negro policemen do not have the consolation of rejecting a role which they themselves find at best uncomfortable. The Negro policeman is forced to play the role of the policeman contrary to his own wishes. He may try to soften the impact of this role by being sympathetic, showing personal interest, or by trying to be friendly. Nevertheless, the essential role remains and he is bound by the stereotype associated with it. The cost of being recognized as a policeman is sometimes quite high.

Ninety percent of them know. It is not the best thing either. I had a '55 Buick. It cost me fifty dollars. I never locked the doors. Some fellow a couple of months ago took the whole ignition out, smashed it and left it out on the street! Purely malicious. And he did it because I am a policeman. (37)

There is also resentment of the policeman's income.

I feel it is good not to be known as a policeman in your neighborhood . . . You get the snide remarks about things that you buy that are new, that is, furnishings, etc. You are not supposed to have anything is their attitude. They also wonder how you got this new item. (38)

Yet it is difficult to ascertain whether they resent his income as reflected in his furnishings, or whether they are responding to him stereotypically as a man who takes graft. Whatever the source of their resentment, however, the result is the same. The Negro policeman seems to be alienated from his neighbors and friends. The result of this alienation is that he tries to conceal his police job from his friends and neighbors so as not to be embarrassed by them or embarrass them by his presence. However, if he is successful in concealing himself in this fashion, it merely increases his feeling of self-alienation.

> Sometimes they get into big discussions with civil rights and they want my opinion as a Negro and as a policeman. And then I discuss it with them. There are times when I wish they didn't know I was a policeman. Perhaps, certain people think that because you are a policeman you are a big man. But I don't want to be a big man, I want to be something else. So if I am at a party and people don't know who I am and they ask me I tell them I am a cab driver or something like that. I don't tell them I am a school teacher. If I told them that they would ask me where do I teach and that would get quite complicated. So I tell them I am a cab driver. (34)

A most pathetic solution is a form of self-imposed isolation.

> I kind of keep away from people. I don't want to get too involved. (29)

> No one can hurt you unless he is your friend. And you won't let people become your friends. (7)

In a few cases the men expressed the feeling that they were not recognized to be policemen. Nevertheless, all of them were quite happy with their anonymity. The same point is made: one can maintain his integrity as a policeman, and his friendship as a Negro, by not disclosing his official status to his friends and neighbors. As one policeman remarked:

> I don't have to be concerned about hurting people's feelings in the sense that you don't want to be a bad fellow. If they knew me as a policeman this would put me in a compromising situation which I don't want. What I mean is this: assuming you have friends in the neighborhood who have invited you to their home and let's say they are doing something that means violating the law. They would expect you to overlook this. If you didn't they would consider this a bastardly act. This way, by not telling them I avoid any action one way or the other. (29)

Because the Negro community is not inclined to receive Negro policemen both as neighbors and friends, Negro policemen tend to form cliques. But since white policemen do not receive Negro policemen into fellowship with them during their off-duty or extra-duty hours, they congregate and fraternize with other Negro policemen. When 30 of these men were asked to list the occupations of their three best friends, 22 listed one Negro policeman among the three. This seems consistent in the light of the uneasy social situations they find in their communities.

Beyond this, the Negro in his official capacity finds himself working on the whole in Negro areas, and sees some virtue in it. When these men were asked, "Is the Negro policeman more effective than the white policeman in a Negro community?" the majority were unequivocal in their positive response. (The official Guardians' position on this question is that there is some virtue in having Negro policemen working in Negro areas as long as it is seen as a "police tactic".) Only a few men qualified their answer. The following quotations bear witness to this.

> Under the present circumstances, yes. Because he has the confidence of the community and he as an individual Negro civilian loses confidence in the white police officer. Consequently the white police officer who has not gained confidence

of the people is not good to that community. Yes I feel he is definitely more effective in a Negro community. Let us face it, you have to have the public's help and if that public doesn't respect you and loses confidence in you, they won't help you. (23)

I am for putting Negro policemen in Negro neighborhoods. A Negro policeman in a Negro neighborhood can communicate the idea that the policeman is a friend instead of an enemy. The black policeman in a black community is definitely much better than putting white policemen there. Negro policemen can bring about a better relationship. (37)

Yes, I do think this. The Negro cop talks to the Negro without talking down to him. It's a self-respecting kind of thing. If you are a criminal you play the game, but the average citizen who is talked to will not feel looked down upon. (17)

I say this: as a Negro I may know my people better than a white individual would know Negro people. And white policemen may know his people better than a Negro policeman. So I think he can be more effective than a white policeman because he is a Negro and knows his people better. (28)

Thus, of the majority who answered in the affirmative, the following rationale is offered: (1) the Negro policeman has the confidence of the Negro community; (2) he is considered a friend and not an enemy; (3) he is more understanding of the problems of the community because he is a Negro; (4) he acts as a buffer between the "brutal white cop" and the Negro citizen; and (5) the general quality of police work is raised by suppressing the handicap of racial prejudice.

THE MIDDLE CLASSES

The above ideology is given reinforcement by the positive image the middle class Negro has of the Negro policeman. Over and over again, these men told of their experiences in Negro communities, and to the question, "What are the attitudes of the Negro community towards Negro policemen?" answered that they are respected and admired by the average, decent, law-abiding Negro citizen. Thus it seems that the Negro policeman draws some personal and social support from the middle-class Negroes in the community. One reason for this is that the amount of his income and the security of his job has prestige in the community. He has "made it" out of the lower depths of the ghetto. The source of income involves prestige because to the middle classes, the Negro policeman has some connection to the non-ghetto world. He gains some authority and prestige of power by even this remote connection to the white world and white power. But he is, unlike the white policeman, accessible to the Negro middle classes. He represents authority without the threatening aspects connected with white policemen. For example:

> Let's talk about the Negro community and its attitudes toward the Negro policeman. If you look at ordinary middle class Negroes and their attitudes in my community there is no adverse dislike for the Negro cop. They have a lot of respect for them—pride for them—glad to see them in uniform. When I went out during the riots they told me to be careful, to take care of myself. They have concern for you. (4)

> Getting back to the average Negro citizen. I think they like to see you. You represent them and most Negro cops are a part of the Harlem community. The white cop gives the Negro citizen that inferior feeling, even though the citizen is not that type of citizen who causes trouble. (17)

Another policeman attributes this support to rapport between Negro policemen and Negro citizens. That is, there is sympathy, or understanding for the other. Of course, one of the uses of understanding is to know when one is being imposed upon.

> To the average citizen I think that the rapport between him and the Negro police officer is much greater than the white police officer. The average Negro citizen can relate much more easily to the Negro officer and more readily to him. (24)

142

And another policeman talked briefly about civil rights as a basis for a correspondence of interests.

> Especially over the last few years where you would have civil rights drives—the average and decent law-abiding citizen is glad to see a Negro policeman. (16)

In contrast to the above, one policeman implies that the relatively few contacts, or episodes, between policemen and middle-class Negroes at the level of control or apprehension, leads to positive or neutral images of police authority. This means that the image of the policeman may be in inverse relation to the distance. The further you are from him the more attractive he is.

> The law-abiding citizen looks at the Negro policeman as a policeman. Matter of fact, he doesn't come into contact with the Negro policeman. And he doesn't care what color you are. There is a certain element we never come into contact with and that is the law-abiding element, whether poor or wealthy. The people you know by name you usually know as law breakers. (38)

The following policeman offers a qualification to this statement. In effect, even among the middle classes, Negro policemen can fall into disrepute.

> Among the many law-abiding—let me put a little dig in here —Negro citizens, there is a somewhat naïve and abstract support of the police officer, regardless of the officer's race. Basically, because they are first of all, law abiding, and as a result, have virtually no contact and thus no conflict with the law. Among the law abiding again, who by virtue of their daily activities (that is, shopping, managing a small business and trying to be conscientious citizens by reporting violations, etc., to the police—and being shocked by what is too often a callous indifference), they have an unquestioned disdain for the police officer (regardless of his race). (10)

The Negro policeman, then, shares with his middle-class clientele an awareness of their mutual interests. He protects them

143

from the criminal element, and in exchange, they grant him prestige in his official role. This keeps his own occupational advancement from seeming like disloyalty to his earlier, more lowly, group status. Thus he is allowed the comfort of confronting the Negro community both as a Negro who has advanced himself, and as a policeman doing a job that is considered vital to the life of the Negro community. In sum, each party has enough mutual interests to allow mutual identification.

THE LOWER CLASSES

The situation is totally different, however, when we consider the lower-class Negro attitudes towards police authority. These policemen told a story of the disrepute into which they fell, the hatred, suspicion, and contempt which they sometimes aroused. The basic theme that runs through their observations is that they are viewed as agents of outside white society—a repressive, discriminatory, anti-Negro society—and are constantly reminded of their Negro identities. Negro policemen are thus vulnerable to charges that they are Uncle Toms or Charlies. For example:

> I think it is pretty negative generally. This stems from the fact that he is a symbol of authority and is a Negro the same as they, and not willing to accede to any leniency that they feel they should have because the police officer is a Negro and they are Negroes. On this basis they would feel that he is not one of them—he has more authority and does not accede to the leniency they demand. Consequently, they feel he is enforcing the white man's law. (12)

In one group interview that was conducted, one policeman acted as a catalyst for the other; some very pointed, harsh, and tragic observations were made.

> *Policeman 1.* In general, the Negro people have a fear and distrust for cops in general. They think of you as being part of the power structure, as an Uncle Tom.

Policeman 2. The Negro community is like the white community. There is no fear of cops. They feel that the policeman is giving them a service that they are paying for. I'm speaking of middle-class Negroes and white people. But the lower classes look at the Negro cop and the white cop as by and large enforcing the property rights of others (whites) and they become the symbol of the power structure.

Policeman 1. You hear sirens going. What does the lower class Negro immediately say? They're going to beat some nigger.

These policemen (3–4) went on to remark:

Policeman 1. In talking with Negroes I have found that many Negroes have a tremendous dislike for cops, and that includes Negro cops. Matter of fact, some of them feel we are worse than the white cops. They respond to the stereotype that Negro cops are tough and this goes back to the old times when the Negro cop was brutal—there is no doubt about it. An incident that comes to my mind was during the World's Fair last year—an incident occurred in the subway and the subway police—the Negro transit police officer started throwing guys off the subways.

Policeman 2. But you're talking about transit police.

Policeman 1. I don't care whether he works as a transit cop or doesn't work as a transit cop. He is still a cop and in this case a Negro cop. You have to be a sort of sadist to be a cop. I really believe that. What people in their right minds would go out and say: I'm going to knock the living shit out of you. Where the cop acts as if he is both judge, jury, high lord, and executioner to hit this guy—to beat him to a pulp. They are cruel! There is undoubtedly a certain degree or percent of sadists in the department.

Policeman 2. You think there is a police mentality then?

Policeman 1. Yes, I do.

To the lower class Negro, the Negro policeman is just a hated "cop."

145

> When I got jumped in a colored community, the Negro peo-
> ple ganged up on me. There was a knifing. I tried to break it
> up. There was one guy who said: Mother fuck the cop. Be-
> fore I know it, I was on the ground. He caused the crowd to
> hit me. I arrested him. (4)

One policeman attributed the negative image received from
Negroes to the lack of respect he received from his own colleagues and the white community at large. In this sense, police
authority rests upon the reinforcement of respect that white colleagues have for each other. When this is not visible to Negro
citizens, they in turn do not give him their respect.

> It's harder for a Negro policeman working in a Negro neigh-
> borhood, no less other Negroes. Why? Since white society
> doesn't openly invite or accept him as a duly fledged officer,
> the Negro civilian with his economic or educational station
> is not expected to give him any more, and does not give him
> any more; and can't be expected to, since his white brothers
> don't—why should he? He is looking at the Negro officer in a
> second class way anyhow. (25)

The southern Negro

The negative esteem that the Negro policeman receives is not
only the result of the attitudes of lower-class Negroes who frequently attempt to discredit him, but also of the specific subgroups he confronts within the lower-class community. There is,
for example, complete agreement among the Negro policemen in
this study that the rural southern migrant who comes to the
North has a particular hatred for policemen, both white and
Negro. These men indicate that this is due to the wholly negative
experiences he has had with southern policemen, involving
blatant police lawlessness or oppressiveness. This is not mere
speculation on their part. Gunnar Myrdal has indicated that the
southern policeman has occupied a crucial position in upholding
the caste system in the South, sanctioned by southern public

opinion and supported by a police administration that not only tolerates offensive conduct on the part of its agents in dealing with Negroes, but condones it.[4] The following typical quotation supports this view.

> To the Negro, the police represents not help but it represents abuse (I'm speaking as a Negro now). And this attitude is carried over down through the ages of what happened previously. Many of the southern Negroes who came up North carried with them the abuse they received from white policemen in the South and act accordingly up North. (2)

The southern Negro particularly hates the *Negro* policeman. This is so because Negro officers in the South have traditionally been restricted to patrolling Negro areas and arresting Negro offenders. Only in rare instances have they been legally allowed to arrest whites. Consequently, many of the experiences that southern Negroes have had with the police have been with Negro policemen. Thus the Negro policeman in the South has come to symbolize the archetype of Uncle Tom. As one informant put it:

> I think the southern Negro citizens are sometimes a little hostile toward you. There is a double standard in the South. One reason for this is because of their experience in the South with cops. And if it is true that a southern Negro cop who works in the South can only lock up Negro citizens in the South, then, they get it from both ends. The southern Negro citizen has a bad experience with Negro cops because the Negro is sent into Negro areas, and he has a bad experience generally with the uniform and white cops. So he gets it from both ends, and he brings this experience up to the North with him. (17)

Because of this, many southern Negroes who come to the North not only distrust the Negro policeman, but avoid him.

[4] For an extended treatment of the southern policeman see Gunnar Myrdal, *An American Dilemma: The Negro Problem and Modern Democracy* (New York, Harper, 1944), pp. 535-545.

They have a tendency not to come to policemen for help, although he may talk more to a Negro policeman than a white policeman. But I would say there isn't that friendly trust. He still looks at you as a policeman and to be wary, but not that wide, friendly hello type of thing. (38)

I have seen by the way where southern Negroes would generally rather go to a white cop than to a Negro cop . . . (33)

Negro youth

The Negro policeman must not only deal with a carry-over value of police brutality and abuse experienced by southern migrants at the hands of southern policemen, but he must also deal with a segment of the hostile motivations from youth which combines hostility toward elders, whites, the middle class, and the establishment. Although older persons in the Negro community may have come to accept police authority, young persons have rarely been able to. Beyond this, law-breaking Negro youths are not professional criminals and thus do not seem to fear police power.

I get abuse from kids. They feel I shouldn't side with a white cop. There are a lot of Negro girls who are just vicious and have some mouth. They are angry because I am a Negro policeman and that I am not helping them. They have called me a white man's nigger. What do you do? You throw them out or lock everybody up. (33)

Another policemen made a similar point.

The teenagers give you the most trouble and the most mouth and call you the most names. Especially the girls—they hide behind their sex and their age to protect themselves from getting hit, and become pretty damn abusive towards us. During the demonstrations we were told to remain impartial. As far as I'm concerned, I am only interested during this time with my personal safety. I tell them to get moving and to keep

148

moving, but you can't talk to some of them, they are like animals. When they act like animals you have to get tough. (8)

The attempt by Negro offenders to evoke the policeman's guilt

The Negro offender is least identified with the established social order and is the most overt in expressing hostility to its agent. He is also the most frequently apprehended person, with the greatest arrest experience, and better known to policemen—both white and Negro—by virtue of this increased contact. In addition, there is not much that he can do against the power of the policeman. Authority is on the side of the cop. The policeman cannot lose, nor can the society remain viable if he loses. And yet the policeman cannot win either, if the result is lawlessness. The issue must remain unresolved. Nevertheless, young Negro offenders tend to create special difficulties for the Negro policeman in carrying out his role. When forty policemen were asked, "Does the Negro offender give you a hard time, or a harder time, than he gives white policemen?" thirty-two of them answered yes. Their replies revolve around a common theme: whenever the Negro policeman attempts to assert his authority those who resent it try to empty it of meaning by (1) calling him a traitor; (2) using him as a "soft touch"; and (3) challenging his authority. This attempt by lower-class violators to impose their social definitions on the Negro policeman invokes some tragic situations both for the offender and the policeman.

One object of provoking the policeman is to force him to back down—that is, to use him as a "soft touch."

It is more like a cry from the community: I am black— you are black. Why are you against me? They do this to me. They do this to you. Why do you molest me? (9)

Yes, a Negro offender will give me a harder time than a white cop. If you stop someone for a traffic violation, the Negro violator will say this to me: How about giving me a break, I'm just like you. How about giving me a break, I'm colored too. When they talk like this, they get a ticket right away. No doubt about it. A real quick summons. (7)

The Negro violator by color association thinks he is going to get a break. A Negro felon on the other hand would resent you but not any more than a white cop. He is trying to avoid being captured. He doesn't think of your color. But the misdemeanant will try to use you as I said. (4)

The Negro policeman who confronts an offender must assert himself as a policeman and define the situation in formal terms; otherwise, he is taken advantage of. As one policeman noted:

They get a feeling when a cop is not going to make an arrest. They just know. When he doesn't take positive action. They know that he is full of bullshit. I remember some Negro teen-agers at the Botanical Gardens. They were told that they would be locked up. But we didn't lock them up. They knew we were bluffing. When they know you are bluffing, they get stronger. If you come to them on the corner and you tell them to please move off the corner, and then you come back again and again and tell them to move off the corner, they know you are fooling and you won't lock them up. If you tell them in a different way—with your tone of voice. If you make strong mannerisms and you know your job, they move. (4)

The central quality, in addition to his personal qualities, or sympathetic nature, that makes a policeman a "soft touch," is the fact that he is a Negro. The offender defines the situation on the basis of color; by presenting him with the phrase "I'm just like you," he conveys to the policeman the attitudes and values of his ethnic peers. But he does much more. He reminds the policeman that he too is Negro, and taunts him for occupying a role which he considers detrimental to the Negro race. Thus the Negro policeman is put in a delicate situation, for if he overly

150

asserts himself as a policeman he is likely to be called a bastard, but if he backs down he may be called chicken. His problem, then, is to maintain his authority as a professional policeman without losing his racial identity.

The Negro offender often challenges the official authority of the policeman. In such situations, the policeman must repress the offender by force in order to maintain his initial definition of the situation. In the face of such challenges, order cannot be established without at least a minimum of unpleasantness, both for the offender and the policeman. One policeman described such a situation.

> That depends on the situation and the type of Negro. There was an incident in 1951. My wife was away visiting her family in St. Louis. I was working four to twelve and I had to pick her up at the airport. I'm saying to myself that I don't want any trouble on this shift. I stop a car that is being driven recklessly. It's Saturday night. At that time we would lock up a person for dangerous driving and not give him a summons. So my intention was to give a summons other than dangerous driving. But the guys in the car who were Negroes were giving me a lot of abuse and called me everything under the sun. I kept having visions of going to night court. We take them to the station house and I fill out the card. This one guy tells me he is going to kick my so and so, and he is going to blow my brains out, etc. So I have to give him an opportunity to kick my behind. Anyhow, unfortunately there was a wagon car to take us to night court, and we just made it there and back in time. This is just the kind of condition you come across. So it depends. (15)

Another policeman offers an explanation for the attempt by Negro offenders to challenge his authority. He states, in effect, that Negro authority is taken as a joke because the offender considers the Negro policeman solely on the basis of the policeman's race. However, when such situations arise, the policeman must strongly assert himself in his official role, for the offender cannot be allowed to establish his definition of the situation. In such cases, the inevitable conflict between the authority of the "cop" and the Negro offender becomes more severe, because the force used by the policeman to maintain his authority merely reinforces his identity as a traitor in the eyes of the offender.

> Unfortunately the Negro throughout the years has respected whites and white authority. And Negroes are unable to accept the same authority when told by a Negro police officer. The Negro policeman to them represents, I suppose, a person who is on the same level as themselves. They can't do what he tells them. If a white police officer is on the scene, they would automatically follow instructions . . . The Negro policeman doesn't have the fear of Negro citizens as they do of white policeman . . . And when a Negro policeman tells them to do something, it is taken more or less in a joking fashion, until enough force is used to change the complexion of the situation. Fear is therefore a very important fact in this . . . And I think fear or the lack of fearing the Negro police officer is vital in answer to your question. (29)

The object of provoking the policeman is to either force him to back down, or force him to act like a Cossack, a quisling, a stool pigeon. In either case the offender has triumphed over the policeman, because he imposes his own negative image upon the policeman, and does not allow the policeman to define the situation ("putting one on" or "jiving"). In either case the offender triumphs even though in the process he may be arrested, beaten up or "shook up." To avoid this the policeman must define the situation in his own terms: make the arrest without anger, even with humor, and not respond in terms of guilt, or defensive aggressiveness. But this requires that he be free from self-hatred or share the hatred of the "cop."

A number of policemen said, in effect, "Negroes feel that I am an Uncle Tom." One policeman offered an explanation for this definition which has been consistently imposed upon the Negro policeman. What is particularly clear in his comments is the element of defensiveness. Some policemen are driven to be abusive.

One attitude may be typified by remarks made over the switchboard by a civilian calling for police aid from a police box on the street. Certainly fifteen to twenty years ago, you could hear this statement: Send me a policeman and don't send me no nigger policeman! This remark came from a Negro complainant! (I knew that would get you.) Why? One way to explain this is that in the earlier days of the history of the Negro policeman, say 1940 or 1945, or before 1940, his position was greatly resented by the lawless element. To the respectable Negro community, it was a considerably high station—primarily because so many avenues through which the average Negro citizen could pursue his potential was tightly closed to the Negro. The knowledgeable Negro knew too what one of his own kind had to go through to become a policeman. Hopefully, more so than now, and there are many manifestations that it was more so than now. The Negro policeman, suffering to a high degree the brainwashing that the race has been subjected to, stereotyped the Negro malefactor, resented his bad reflections upon our people, and too often gave vent to his feelings, and whipped the hell out of the citizen, as badly if not worse than would have the white officer. It must be remembered, that as part of the result of this brainwashing, there was a widely spread subservient attitude that was unconsciously succumbed to, regardless of the overt expression on the Negroes' part to the contrary. In a sense, the Man, or, Mr. Charlie, or, the Boss, had more of a right to deal with the Negro malefactor than any uppity, or smart-aleck Negro officer. Now one way of resolving this dilemma would be to look upon the Negro officer as a goddamn stooge for the white man. (10)

It seems from his analysis, then, that the Negro policeman becomes the scapegoat for the underprivileged Negro who displaces the burden of his own misfortunes upon the policeman. By condemning the Negro policeman, the Negro malefactor compensates for his subservient position to the white man. Whether Negro policemen as a whole overreact in their dealings with Negro offenders, as this policeman claims, will now be discussed.

The reactions of Negro policemen to the provocations of the Negro offender

The guilt-evoking mechanisms described constitute a threat to the adjustment of the Negro policeman to his occupational role. Thus the Negro policeman develops techniques to secure and maintain his authority as a policeman in the face of diverse challenges. With this point of view, these men were asked, "Are Negro policemen more tough with Negro offenders than with white offenders?" The answers to this question were almost equally divided between two types of response: (1) those whose reactions exhibited a hard or Cossack approach to the provocations of the offender; and (2) those whose reactions did not consider their role to be defined in these terms (being hard or soft). The hardliners typically view the offender in terms of his race. When confronted with situations which require them to make an arrest, they not only react to the offense, but to the offender's race as well as their own. They justify their hardness simply because offenders attempt to embarrass them on racial grounds. In fact, they resent that attempt to embarrass them as much as the crime itself. Those who do not consider their role as such, respond on the whole in terms of what the offender has done, is doing, or is expected to do; ignoring race both in terms of sympathy with or overreaction to the offender. This type of policeman carries out his role in a strict, formal way as defined by his professional status, and is not influenced by membership in a particular group. For both types we would observe that reactions to the Negro offender are part of the policeman's personality, the way he defines his role, and a function of his general social adjustment to the situation as defined by the offender.

The following hardliners justified their hardness simply because offenders attempted to embarrass them, especially in the presence of white policemen.

> Yes, under certain circumstances I'm more tough. If I feel I can do more to help him by being harsh. But I'm even more tough if they try to embarrass me. I have been embarrassed

by Negro offenders, by their behavior and calling me names in front of white police officers. If I'm with a Negro cop and they call me names, it doesn't bother me. But with a white cop it is embarrassing. I like to talk to the people and make them aware of the law, especially if they are poor and it's a minor violation. I let them off easy . . . I really get mad at juveniles and adolescents. Young offenders, dropouts, gangs trying to terrify a neighborhood. I have in mind the summer in Harlem. I feel they are wasting their time, their lives—five to ten years from now they still will be out there in the streets. (5)

One policeman, responding in terms of the offender's race, goes beyond the call of duty in making an arrest.

There are a lot of Negroes, the only thing they understand is a boot in the right direction. They are not different than a lot of children. The only thing they understand is physical force and pain. When you meet that type you have to give it to them—but you have to distinguish one from the other. I remember an incident in Brownsville: there was this leader of the gang there, and I saw him striking his aunt right in front of the steps leading to the subway. Now you don't act this way, so this was the excuse I was looking for. I got out of the car and told him he was under arrest. He said he wasn't going. I gave him a shot in the gut and threw him into the patrol car. I didn't take him to the precinct, but I drove him around the neighborhood in the patrol car so his friends could see what had happened to him (the tough leader). After driving around for a while, I stopped the car and took him into an alley and beat the hell out of him. I told him if I saw him acting up again this way, I would put a bullet through him. That was the end of his leadership days. He no longer got into trouble that I know of. (14)

He continued:

So in answer to your question, those I have to be, I would be more tough with. Surprisingly, all of the arrests that I have made have had no trouble. The first approach you use is the

> most impressive. You learn to size up a situation first time you walk into the situation. One kid gave me some lip in a store and I said, "All right, you've had it." He said to me that he wasn't going. I said, "You don't mean you're not going to go—it's just how you're going to go." In other words, this type of man—is the only thing he understands and many of these types you have to hit so he knows you actually mean this. (14)

Such reactions grow out of the contradictory definitions of the situation. The resolution that these men have found is to inflict physical punishment. This punishment is perceived under the circumstances as necessary to maintain their authority and respect as police officers in the presence of offenders who try to embarrass them. Unfortunately, such reactions can only add to the negative image that "cops" already hold in the eyes of Negroes.

Such tragic situations for both the policeman and the offender were confirmed by another police officer.

> I have treated many Negroes in a way I wouldn't treat a dog. I am harder on a Negro that commits an infraction of the law than a white person who commits an infraction. Why? It's because [pointing to a chair] I know that where that chair is there are a few people raising hell. But another group are quiet and not raising their voices. The first group will scream and shout and raise all kinds of noise. Now, I will chase these people off the corner. Now by the time the other people see me they will have started to move off the corner. I go up to this second group and tell them that I have to chase them too. I am making an explanation to one type of group and not the other. This is what you run across. I recognize that many of them need education, training, have inferior schools, mothers and fathers may be someplace else. I try to put everything into a certain category, which is probably wrong. I have to judge a man by the way I find him, and I am particularly hard on a person who creates a problem. (15)

When asked to further explain the differences of treatment, this officer continued:

Well, if a Negro person is doing something, he is kicking me in the behind. The white person is not kicking me in the behind but society in the behind. So with the civil rights movement this particular man is a drawback, and to rehabilitate this man I think is impossible. (15)

This interpretation, however, evokes negative reactions among other Negro officers. For example, one policeman attributed the following motivations for this type of behavior.

A Negro police officer may be like a reformed drunk. A reformed drunk is harder on drunkards than the average person is on drunks. Where he would see his own reflection of something that he has been trying to get away from. He may see this reflection in the sense that these people are holding down the cause, and that these people are perpetuating the stereotype image of the Negro which he has been trying to lessen, either through education or other means. (29)

Another policeman presented the case even more strongly.

We have Uncle Toms in our race. We call them tail kissers. You have Negro policemen who are ashamed of their own color. They say: I can't see why black people can't act white. They are always smiling, they say. Why can't they stop that, they say. I tell them because that's the way they are. Now that's the black cop I have noticed. And he will lock you up faster than anything, and he feels he is doing the city a great thing. (30)

Yet we must be careful not to place too much stress on such interpretations. In fact, this may not be a question of racial self-hate, but may represent an identification with race in terms of taking pride in Negro achievements, while at the same time losing personal involvement with the Negro struggle. This seems to be well-illustrated by the following situation.

Let me give you a case in point. A Negro says to a white fellow that he wants a dime. The white man ignores him and

157

continues walking. The Negro kid calls the white man a mother fucker. I see this incident. I am in a radio car and in plainclothes. I get out of the car and tell the Negro kid that I am a policeman and to come over. At that time my partner was white. I wanted to give this kid a lesson in civil rights. I take him into the precinct and take my gun off and I tell him that I will beat the living hell out of him. He starts to cry and tells me that he doesn't fight his race. I tell him that doesn't he know that he is killing his race by doing things like that. I take a quarter out and say, "Now here is two dimes. Does that make you feel better? Why in the hell did you ask a white man for a dime and then swear at him for not giving you a dime? You have embarrassed yourself and my race and then you resort to this vernacular. This is the thing that burned me and upset me. I will see you go as far as you want." But without his help in becoming aware of the problem, I am in trouble! But this is the element of the uneducated group —not people in the know. (19)

Another policeman justified his toughness on the grounds that he is concerned for the welfare of the Negro community.

When I worked in Harlem there was an incident I recall. I was working up there when they were having trouble with Adam Clayton Powell telling the people not to buy from liquor stores until they hire Negroes to work there. I remember one Saturday I was working at 126th Street between 7th and 8th Avenues. There was a big crap game going on in the middle of the block (I was just up there for this detail). A radio car with two white officers stopped in front of the game. One person from the game went up to the car and spoke for a bit and the car finally drove away. I walked up there and broke the game up. They gave me some lip about it. I told them to the effect: Let me tell you something. This two-year-old boy watching you play crap is going to be just like you some day or worse than you are someday. You try doing what you are doing in the Man's neighborhood. Grow up! Why am I telling you this? Because I am part of you and I am not going to let you destroy your neighborhood, nor my neighborhood. One man ended up saying, "The officer is right." (14)

158

Whatever the reasons for being tough, the outcome is the same. These men define the situation chiefly in reference to race, and adjust to the provocations of the offender by strongly asserting their authority as policemen. In fact, they become more than policemen; they become moral lessons for their race, even when they use white middle-class standards.

The second group of accommodators see race as an inconsequential factor in their behavior. They feel that police work should be kept as far as possible on an impersonal basis. This is the "professional" policeman who gives nothing and asks nothing of personalities. His is bureaucratic and objective, ignoring race both in terms of sympathy and overreaction. The prototype for this group remarks that an impersonal approach prevents conflict created by the mutual abrasion of racial statuses, allows the policeman to carry out his official role without emotion, and gives the offender the opportunity to respond to the uniform and not the man.

> I'm not hard on either. I don't see my role as being harsh on anybody . . . I never have any feelings of being too hard or too soft on white or Negro offenders. In making an arrest, I make it as painless and as brief as possible. This is for my own self-protection and to keep me from being involved. You can fall for this—you can become emotional about a situation—an arrest. If you become emotional, this hampers your role as a police officer and this is no good. I have been involved in situations where the Negro subject to detention was quite extremely emotional, and he would give me his long trail of trouble of being a Negro, his long suffering, and his sad story. I don't think he knew what the long trail was to be a Negro, but he used this only for his own selfish reasons. When the party is overemotional, I respond by being objective—so long as there is no physical threat to me. (9)

Nevertheless, this policeman went on to remark that it is not easy to separate "the role of the policeman and feelings about my race." In fact, the professional policeman can easily become a hardliner.

159

In Selma, regarding the death of the Negro boy. My reaction has been to shoot them down as mad dogs would be shot down. I reacted to this while I was performing my duties in New York. I said to this white person (actually I said this to myself), please raise your voice to me, please clench your fist —just give me an excuse to brutalize you. This feeling I had was during the time that fellow was killed in Selma. I'm not one to get involved, but this one time it nearly got in my way in my role as a police officer. The incident: A white citizen was fighting a Negro citizen. I approached the scene. The Negro had a bottle that was broken at the top, and the white had a garbage container top. They were prepared to throw it to each other. I didn't feel the racial bit at this moment. I told them to drop it. The Negro did, but the white didn't, possibly because he saw me as a Negro. It became verbal, and I became verbal, and I proceeded to walk him for a block or so—not to harass, but to get him away, and I sent the Negro in a different direction. The Negro responded quickly. The white responded slowly. I told him to make his way homeward or to Broadway somewhere. I don't react professionally to a threat. My professional reaction is: sticks and stones will break my bones, but . . . Then I got aware of this racial feeling through the interplay of words, and I became racially incensed, and this could have affected my performance as a police officer. (9)

THE NEGRO POLICEMAN AND
THE CIVIL RIGHTS MOVEMENT

Much has been written about the civil rights movement, its ideals, goals, leaders, and its impact on a stratified society with conflicting class interests. Yet virtually nothing is known about what effects, if any, the movement has had on the Negro policeman in exercising his official role while maintaining his interest in the cause. Our concern in this section is to develop some hypotheses regarding the following questions: to what extent and degree does the Negro policeman consider himself a part of the struggle? Has the movement created problems for him as a police officer? What are these problems? Does he feel that he has become a traitor to his race because he is a policeman?

The internal conflict

All of the Negro police officers in this study were highly conscious of the civil rights movement. More significant, however, is the theme that emerges from the various replies to the question, "What problems, tensions, conflicts, has the civil rights movement caused for the Negro policeman?" The overall reactions can be stated in these general terms: the Negro police officer is conscious of a moral dilemma. As a Negro, he is in sympathy with the movement, automatically bound up in the problems, thinking, and attitudes that accompany demonstrations. He finds it difficult to take warranted police action against his people, as he is in sympathy with their reasons for making police action necessary. Thus, as a police officer, he realizes that he must bear the burdens of repressing the movements—which sometimes lead to riots, provocations, and violence—movements with which he is basically in sympathy, even though he may object to their specific form and the particular group in question. The following policemen commented in these terms, when asked if the movement had created problems for the Negro police officer:

> Yes, it has. The problem is that you feel the movement as a Negro and you know that it is good for your people, your race, and your country. And at the same time you have to enforce laws on the demonstrators and during these times your heart beats out for them. You have a dual feeling. Especially if you are assigned in front of a school and you know in your heart that the situation exists, because you went to these schools. (38)

> It's the role of most Negro policemen. You have a lot of Negro cops whose mother is on that line, or sister in on the line out there. The Negro cop is out to do a job. When

161

ordered to make an arrest, he makes an arrest—and he tries to be as courteous as possible. We are out there—it's a bitter pill to swallow. We would like to be on the picket line, would like to be out there, because our heart is out there. But our minds have to be on the job even though our feelings are definitely with them. (6)

A conflict is created between the claims of the department and his superiors, and the claims of his conscience. This is especially true because he perceives that Negro policemen are potentially used as instruments of pressure against the demonstrators.

There are many white bosses who would tell a Negro policeman to lock them up. I don't know why he was doing this. Whether he was harassing the Negro cop or wanted to prevent problems, feeling that the Negro cop, because he is a Negro, could be more helpful to the situation. I don't know. (6)

Although it is difficult to ascertain with any reliability the reasons for using Negro policemen in this way, all policemen agree that they are especially used in tense race situations. One policeman presented the case quite bluntly when he said:

His superiors or commanding officer who put him in the front line with the crowd (actually they throw the Negro cop at the rioters), do this on the theory that it's so much better to see a Negro cop beating a Negro demonstrator than a white cop beating a Negro. Because a white cop beating a demonstrator makes for bad press releases. So you find the Negro cop, who has to detail a riot, in a bad situation. (18)

Whether he is being used in the terms he describes is not the issue. The issue is that he perceives a conflict between his feelings and attachments to the cause of civil rights and the demands of his job. Yet because he earns his living as a policeman, he has no choice but to carry out the commands of his superiors during these racial demonstrations. He may justify this

162

uncomfortable role on the grounds of being a professional "cop." For example:

> The Negro cop limits his action to actual violations of law, and he has to detach himself from the emotional aspect of the situation. He concentrates on the actual violation of law, or attempts to prevent a violation of law. At least he tells himself that he is doing this. (18)

Whatever the justification, he suffers with a police role he finds distressing in situations regarding civil rights demonstrations. One policeman, who spoke for most of these men, expressed this moral dilemma explicitly.

> I am in a ticklish situation. How so? Let's say I have to decide if I am going to be a policeman first or a Negro first. If I am a policeman first, I ostracize the other Negroes. If I am a Negro first, there goes my job. So I don't know. (36)

Another policeman offered some rationalizations for carrying out a police policy he finds distasteful.

> They had demonstrated opposite King County Hospital. We fared worse than the white policeman. But I had to keep in my mind that I was a police officer. I would say that if you don't enforce the law, this place would become a jungle. I had to keep reminding myself this during those demonstrations. But seeing what the people were doing and observing the nastiness of the white policemen, this hurt me badly. I couldn't sleep for a few days. We felt, if we were to be put in the position of brutalizing our own people, then we would have to hand in our shields. But we felt that we were doing the right thing then. (37)

He went on to comment:

> For the good of my own people you have to remember you are a Negro at all times. You have to try to do a job. I have locked up a million Negroes as far as that goes. But I am a Negro

first, and that is all there is to it. When it comes to protect life and property of all individuals, I am a police officer. But when it comes to protect civil liberties, I am just a Negro. (37)

This may be overstating the moral dilemma facing most Negro policemen. Actually, the dilemma has been resolved by definition and in the fashions outlined in the responses. Those who have survived as policemen have resolved the conflict simply by carrying out their orders. These conflicts are central facts of life to which the Negro policeman has learned to adjust. This may suggest that as a *type*, this policeman is trying to be both a Negro and a policeman. He does this by expressing his discomfort in being a Negro in a series of private conversations, yet suppresses these feelings of racial identity while in the line of his official duty. The internal conflict which is resolved on the front lines of the demonstrations expresses itself in guilt feelings in doing a job which he is economically dependent on, but finds psychologically distressing.

In this connection it is necessary to add that a minority of policemen did not even acknowledge privately that there is a moral dilemma. They see themselves exclusively as cops and do not feel they are straddling both sides of the issue. Their rationale for not feeling this dilemma can be stated in four general propositions: (1) the Negro policeman takes action regardless of how much or how little he may be in sympathy with the cause—the civil rights movement and his role as a police officer are mutually exclusive; (2) only as a civilian does he identify with the cause; (3) he participated in the March on Washington in a professional capacity—to assist in the control of their demonstrations by serving as escorts for the dignitaries, parade guides, and to some extent as advisors. The civil rights organizations thus recognized the service they could render to the movement as policemen; and (4) they reflect the Guardian ideology on this issue, which is that the policeman must realize that all the conscientious and knowledgeable civil rights demonstrators want to do is, if necessary, to be civilly disobedient in order to dramatize their cause, and that such a person expects that the police officer will perform his duty objectively and therefore impartially.

When both types of policemen were confronted by the question, "do you feel you have violated civil rights (or have been disloyal to the cause) because you are a policeman?" all policemen, except one, were unequivocal in their negative responses. The isolated case expressed the possibility of this being so:

> I've got a job to do! I've got to go out and earn money, to pay the mortgage. I try to do the job to the best of my ability. I try to treat people as people. That is about all I can say. (36)

The movement may bring about ambivalence, but it does not mean transgression of one's allegiances simply because one is a police officer. One policeman seemed to be talking for all policemen when he said:

> Basically his loyalties are with the department because he wants to protect his job and position. There are not too many outspoken Negro policemen. They have to conceal their emotions—they have to swallow their pride because if you are outspoken, you are considered by superiors and white policemen as troublemakers. (2)

One cynical policeman made the remark that many Negro policemen have no devotion to the cause of civil rights, nor any feelings of responsibility to the movement, because they are self-interested and self-seeking men.

> I doubt it whether the Negro policeman feels disloyal. There are many Negro cops who are not interested in people but themselves. So this idea of disloyalty doesn't bother him at all. Then another kind of Negro cop feels this is the only way you are going to achieve anything, through demonstrations. If he has the get-up-and-the-go he feels he could do more by participating in the demonstrations. But you can't join the organizations if you are in the police department. (14)

165

All in all, the response to the question on loyalty was a defensive one, and made it extremely difficult for policemen to express themselves. One police officer accurately questioned the appropriateness of such a question by saying, "Do you think a Negro policeman would answer that question if he did feel this?"

We can conclude that the civil rights movement, at worst, has created an internal conflict for the majority of Negro policemen, while at the same time there is no evidence that this ambivalence has been in any way debilitating to them in their professional capacity. Although no officer would admit that he had transgressed the civil rights movement, this does not mean that police officers do not feel they have violated the movement. Perhaps it is only that no way was found to elicit this information in the interviews. Yet we can surmise that the professional role of the policeman involves objective, professional behavior that overrides personal, subjective, nonprofessional loyalties. In dealing with these objective standards the Negro policeman must either repress his personal loyalties and commitments which relatively few do (some overreact by being tougher on Negro offenders than white policemen would be), repress the knowledge of a conflict as many do, or temporarily suspend from consciousness those nonprofessional sentiments which interfere with their police role. This is especially true if the policeman is economically dependent on his job, as of course most policemen, black and white, are.

The external conflict

A clear-cut illustration of the double role contradiction of the Negro policeman was the recent controversial issue of a nonjudicial civilian review board independent of police authority. It will be recalled that for the Negro community the civilian review board was considered the last defense against "police rioting against Negroes," and a forum in which their grievances could be heard, and hopefully, implemented. To the white police or the Patrolmen's Benevolent Association the creation of a civilian review board would "impair morale" and discourage "vigorous performance of duty." More significantly, perhaps, the establishment of such a board, external to police administrative authority, was viewed by the police as interfering with the professional autonomy of law enforcement. Particularly offensive was the feeling that police agencies were singled out while many other agencies of government, such as the Transit Authority police, and the Housing Authority police, were not to be affected. Lastly, from the point of view of the P.B.A., the citizen with a legitimate grievance already had easy access to a number of legally constituted agencies, including the Human Rights Commission, the Department of Justice, the Attorney General, and the courts.

The Black Guardians, while having an occupational identity with their white colleagues, clearly rejected the discriminatory suggestions that were made during the campaign, which conveyed to the nation that there was a "black menace" and "New Yorkers could no longer walk without fear" if such a board were to be instituted. The Guardians publicly announced their support of a civilian review board, and by doing so affirmed their identity with the Negro community and their allegiance to one of the goals of the civil rights movement.

Unfortunately, the Guardians' statement only added another element of stress to a situation hitherto characterized by ambivalence, ambiguity, and conflict. Prior to the Guardians' announcement the Negro policeman could handle whatever feelings of moral conflict he had to the civil rights groups by either repressing any knowledge of conflict or by "bracketing out" those nonprofessional sentiments which would interfere with his official role. But as a result of the Guardians' position the Negro policeman was now faced with the charge of being disloyal to his white working companions. In this regard, the president of the Patrolmen's Benevolent Association was reported to have said: "I think they—(the Guardians)—cut right down a color line and it is unfortunate they put their color before their duties and their oath as policemen."[5] The irony of the statement rests on the fact that

[5] As reported in the New York *Amsterdam News*, July 2, 1965.

Negro policemen have higher integrity and greater loyalty to the department than they have been given credit for.

Let us review some of the comments made by Negro policemen regarding the Guardians' position. (It should be noted that the majority of Negro policemen on an individual basis were principally in agreement with the Guardians' statement.)

> The statement that was put out by the Guardians Association about the civilian review board and the fact that the majority of the Negro policemen supported this. There has been some dissension among Negro policemen regarding the statement and some feel that a clique within the Guardians Association did this. Personally, most of the guys who have expressed this are windbag guys anyhow. That is, some of these guys who are against the statement made by the Guardians. The type of guys who have this attitude: the Guardians is a bullshit organization because many went to the Guardians for a particular detail and they didn't get it. They are angry at the Guardians for some personal reason that happened to them some time ago, but the reasons are really trivial in this situation. However, even though they disagreed with the Guardians putting the statement out, they did not disagree with the content of the statement. (32)

The key sentence is that they agreed with the "content" of statement but not with the public announcement. However, the motivations that this man attributes to other Negro policemen for disagreeing with the announcement do not correspond with the majority view. In fact, they contradict his own comments on the matter. When asked why they were against the statement, he answered: "They feel that now they will get into trouble. That the white bosses will be a little hard on them." He then went on to confirm this regarding his own personal feelings on the matter:

> On this issue I really don't know. I don't know which way to go. I agree with the statement but this might make the bosses vindictive towards me. If I want to get a cup of coffee they may put me up for charges just for that. They can do

that you know. So I don't know what to say. I think it's made things a little rougher for the Negro cop, that's for sure. (32)

Such a response reflects ambivalence regarding the Guardians' statement. While agreeing with the need for a civilian review board, he was unhappy about the fact that support of it was publicly announced because his loyalties to the department are now questioned by his white counterparts. Another policeman offered some similar ideas:

I would say it put some people in an uncomfortable situation. When you realize that the majority of the white police officers were against it. We are a minority and because of our color we are visible. And being visible we stand out. So the statement made us stand out that much more. The Guardians' statement was a reflection of a general feeling that Negro policemen are second-class citizens. People in the Negro community feel there are grounds for police brutality. I don't believe this myself, but the people feel there are grounds for this. And being a Negro, I identify with them and their cause. (41)

The Negro policeman can no longer enjoy even the luxury of being considered an exception. He now is visible as an *organized* group to white policemen. Another policeman remarked on this dilemma:

The policemen were angry and unhappy about this. Because we are all individuals. I was against it as a policeman— against the civilian review board. But when I consider it as a Negro cop I am more for it than against it. Also, some of the guys were afraid of the repercussions of such a statement on their jobs, details, and the harassment they might get. (34)

All of these statements suggest that regardless of their economic mobility and integration in the police department they were second-class policemen. They were accepted as long as they let the white policeman do the talking. The Guardians' statement exposed them to reprisal because they had become uppity, had

169

dared to disagree.[6] They have integrated jobs only if they don't disagree. Becoming a policeman then is an economic move rather than an escape from social powerlessness.

Although the Guardians publicly declared that the decision of Negro policemen to support a civilian review board had been made by them after "lengthy and sober reflection," the irony of the statement falls with greater impact on those Negro police officers who were in fact *against* the civilian review board. In this connection Negro policemen were put in the position of defending themselves against a statement which did not reflect their opinions. Nevertheless, they are treated equally as guilty as those who voted for it simply because they are Negroes. The following statement is typical for this minority view.

> We are angry about the statement. We are cops too! We come across the same things that white cops come across. Some of the people who get pushed around deserve it. The best way to handle some guys is to punch them in the mouth . . . When you have to make a decision in a split second you can't have a body of people to decide whether this is police brutality. There are instances where I can see a review board actually changing the nature of the job . . . I think that a prerequisite for a person becoming a member of the review board—the civilian should ride in a radio car and see what is going on. He should work in a detective squad for a time and see what is happening. How can a man evaluate your actions unless he understands the conditions under which you work? That is my question. I think that is very important here. (34)

Implicit in the preceding discussion is the conclusion that the police role is often incompatible with a racial role. Indeed, this assumption is the function of certain personal and social configurations he confronts in the community in which he works. But the contradiction of being both a Negro and a policeman is not resolved by being promoted to a plainclothes status, but merely shifted to a different context.

[6] In the light of these statements, it is interesting to note the recent emergence of black nationalism in the formation of the New York Society of Afro-American Policemen.

= 7

The uniform

The police uniform is a symbol of the authority, power, and legal status of the police. To the population at large, it symbolizes the right of the policeman to exercise power including violence, if necessary. To the policeman it confirms his official authority, and affirms whatever motives he had for becoming a policeman. Beyond this it separates him from the civilian population. It places distance between him and that population, the distance being not only that of the official meaning of the uniform, but a crystallization of all the attitudes that both police and civilians have towards the police.

The above is true for both white and Negro policemen, but the meanings invested in the uniform of the Negro policeman by both Negro and white policemen and Negro and white civilians are different for the Negro policeman than they are for the white.

171

THE UNIFORM AS A PUBLIC TARGET

Negro policemen, when asked the question, "What does the police uniform mean to you?" looked at the uniform as a target of ridicule, scorn, abuse, and derision, from both the Negro and white communities, and from whites in the department. A few imputed a positive meaning to it, and no one among the group was indifferent to it. In addition, almost all of them were eager to get out of it. They tend to call the uniform a "bag" or a "monkey suit" (other policemen have called it the "blues," "formal," "gear," and "kit").

To rename the uniform a "bag" or "monkey suit" is a clue to a reassessment of the Negro policeman's relation to it. The values that might be attributed to it, such as residual blame or responsibility—"holding the bag"—are not in the uniform but in the judgments and evaluations of its wearer. Thus the uniform as an acquired symbol allows us to see how the Negro policeman feels he is perceived and evaluated by the public and the department, in addition to giving us some information on how the Negro's self-image is affected by wearing the uniform.

Of the majority group that attributed negative meanings to the uniform two different types of negative opinion were expressed: (1) most of the policemen identified the uniform with authority, and they rejected the uniform because they did not want to accept the authority implied by that uniform; (2) some policemen made the point that wearing a uniform is a symbol of working at the lowest level—that is, being a detective is a promotion. Thus, for this group, the rejection of the uniform could be considered a rejection of the low position they occupy relative to other positions that are available in the department, not therefore, in itself a rejection of the police role.

Some evidence that those policemen who rejected the wearing of the uniform in a job that requires a uniform also rejected the authority and the official identity of their police role is given in the following statements:

172

I would like to get out of the uniform. After eight hours I do get out of the uniform. I get out and my job ends there. Like I say, if you go back years the uniform is a form of authority and people will resent it, and it doesn't matter who is behind the uniform. People will resent authority. So the uniform represents authority on the whole and this is a limitation to the public to what they can do. Because of the limitation to what they can do, there is a gap between the public and the policeman. (28)

The Youth worker could not conceivably think of wearing a uniform when he is on his assigned tour of duty. A Youth worker, after all, must convey the image that he is performing a service, not exercising an authority role which the uniform symbolizes.

It makes the job more pleasant when you are not wearing a monkey suit. If you are working with youths—it looks like hell if you go up to Mrs. Jones in a monkey suit. This would alarm the neighbors. If you go up to Mrs. Jones in civilian clothes this doesn't arouse any curiosity among the neighbors. Another factor is that when you are in uniform you are always in the position to be stopped by someone to render a service or some other duty, other than the one you are assigned to do. You are, in addition, always subject to constant supervision in uniform. These are the reasons that most guys want to get out of the bag. (18)

Another policeman's typical reaction to the meaning of the uniform is a way of rejecting the identification of being a policeman. In this negative identification lies the fear that he too will become that which he finds humiliating.

I don't like wearing it. I am ashamed of it! It is like walking with a neon sign hanging on your head all the time. The public has brought this feeling upon us. They way the public looks upon us that we are all grafters. None of us like the bag. Most of us are ashamed to admit we are police officers when we are off duty and that is a fact! And this is due to the negative feeling that the public—Negro and white—has of

173

> us and because of this feeling it can't be a profession. You
> are always telling people what they can't do. That is pretty
> hard to take for some people. And working with a public
> that is negative toward you day in and day out doesn't make
> you feel too good about the job you know. (38)

Such a response suggests that simply because of his uniform, he becomes an open and vulnerable target to public observation, examination, and criticism. He becomes imbedded in the common emblematic order of "the police" by virtue of the fact that the civilian population reacts to him in a particular manner. He comes to be known by what he can do and what he represents in his official capacity, and his uniform is the symbol of his right to exercise the power vested in his office. While Negroes need have no sense of shame about displaying the legitimate mark of their official status, this policeman strongly indicates that he is put into the paradoxical position of defending his integrity as a policeman, while sharing the self-hatred of the "cop."

A reinstatement of the requirement that policemen travel to and from work in uniform was introduced in the summer of 1964 as one measure to combat heavy increases in crime. However, the order was withdrawn in September of that year after pressure from the Patrolmen's Benevolent Association. The reasons given by the Association were basically in agreement with comments such as this one.

> The wearing of the uniform to and from work was rescinded.
> Most of the policemen circumvented this ruling anyhow. It
> was a ridiculous rule. You would end up getting to work late
> and being tremendously delayed going home because some-
> one would see you and stop you to ask you questions, and as
> long as you have it on you are on the job. And all these delays
> you weren't compensated for. (39)

This is an interesting comment. In uniform the public sees you in your official role; it doesn't recognize you as an individual. If you want to be an individual or if you don't want to face the public in a public role, that is, reject your official identity, you get out of uniform.

Another policeman who also rejects the official identity he occupies placed this in the context of being vulnerable to "accusations."

> Once you work in uniform you are given a certain area. You are fixed in a certain area of responsibility. You can't duck this responsibility. He is conspicuous because of the presence of the uniform. Secondly, anyone who doesn't like the policeman, the poor guy in uniform is a sitting duck for him. The guy can say that an incident occurred in this particular area and that the policeman abused him. The policeman can't say he wasn't there. They can't hide. They absolutely want to get out of uniform. Here I am talking about being wrongfully accused of something so this is characteristic of the job and the uniform adds to this. (21)

The following responses are typical of those few policemen who felt that wearing a uniform is a symbol of working at the lowest level. They want to take a job that does not require a uniform, a job that is a high level job indicating mobility in the department (being a detective is a promotion). Thus for this group the uniform is rejected because of the low level of work it symbolizes.

> To get out of uniform is a status symbol. To get out of uniform is to get a detail, and it means that you have arrived. It is a step up, a mark in the department. For example, the detectives, plainclothes, are all marks in the department. Also, not wearing a uniform means you wear a tie and a shirt and you feel like a gentleman. To show you the step up: when you do something bad you are going back into the bag. (1)

> The uniform is an attraction to the public—to get help, to get aid and information. But most guys would like to get out of the uniform. A big reason for wanting to become a detective is to get out of uniform. (2)

> The Detective Bureau is a good thing—you're out from under supervision—certain prestige inside and outside of the job.

Even when you meet the public as a detective there is a big difference. Even on a job where the uniform men get there first, the attitudes toward them are different. The detective division personnel are thought of as the brains. The cop is a flatfoot, and doesn't have the brains. Getting out of uniform is a good thing—it means you have moved up. (3)

Only three policemen showed a strong liking for the uniform. One of these men commented on the problem of differentiating between agencies because of the similarity in the uniform, and this is cause for some concern, particularly because he identifies with the uniform. He noted:

Also other civil service jobs have similar uniforms—guards look like policemen, etc. You should have only New York City policemen wearing the blue uniform. And the other agencies should wear a different uniform. Many times a civilian will see some guy in blue drunk, or sleeping or what have you, and from the distance you don't know whether this guy is a city policeman or not. And you get a bad name this way. (5)

The second of these men who identified with the uniform stated: "I love working in uniform because I am able to show the people what a policeman should stand for and what he can do." The other policeman did not so much indicate an acceptance of the police identity as much as his own vanity: "I enjoy wearing it. I am sort of military so I like it in this sense."

One young policeman calls our attention to the need to be affiliated with some superpersonal entity, something larger than oneself as a Negro. He finds this in identifying with the police.

When I first came in on the job I loved the uniform! I belonged to something worthwhile. I'll never forget the first day that I came to my precinct—it was a rainy day. I was so proud wearing that shiny uniform. I spent eight hours on the street. I was hoping somebody would see me. Let's face it no cop spends eight hours on the street. He is always taking a break

> some place for coffee, etc. But I spent the full eight hours on the street. I walked and walked. I was proud. (37)

However, the realities of police work have prevented him from satisfying this need to identify with the uniform. The result is a kind of ambivalence regarding both the cause of his present disillusionment with the job, and his identification with the police role. He continued:

> I don't feel this way now. Although I haven't been on the force very long you can live a lifetime in a short time. I don't have the same kick. I am a little mixed up now. I am trying to figure things out. I didn't first think it was the work, but now I do. Reasons? I don't know. I think a lot of pressures within the department. I think the civil rights movement has created certain pressures. I think there is a backlash at work in the department. And the fact that you have to give a certain amount of summonses. And the image we have put out ourselves. The image is not the best. The policemen have not lived up to the image I gave you of a good policeman. (37)

Nevertheless, the Negro policeman as a Negro has an identity of his own independent of his police uniform. He is still a member of an ethnic category visible as such, and is responded to in these terms apart from other considerations, except when he is identified as a special kind of Negro, one who happens to wear a uniform. In this case, the Negro policeman is subject to double jeopardy, that is, negative evaluations. He must suffer not just from the negative images of the police and the poor image of the department; he also suffers from racial prejudice.

> The policeman is a minority, and the Negro is also a minority. The policeman is visible because of his uniform and so is the Negro because of his color. So when you combine the two, it doubles the two forms of discrimination. (41)

Different negative attitudes are experienced from a white or a Negro public. But regardless of this fact, the policeman faces, in different combinations, the essential role contradictions that stem from his double identity. The uniform which signifies authority is viewed by whites as incompatible with his being Negro. Indeed, the assumption of status incongruence dictates the conclusion that the Negro who works for a white public is often not considered worthy of his new police role.

> The negative features of being a Negro policeman are the same as being a Negro citizen in New York City. It's just the same, much less the fact that the Negro patrolman has the right to enforce the law which makes things worse. If there is any hate regarding you as a citizen (and of course there is plenty in this city) the hate will be double when you have authority. They say a Negro and authority! That's pretty hard to take. (25)

In addition, that the police role shall be satisfying requires not only that it should meet economic requirements and be deemed appropriate by the person occupying it, but also that it should be respected by others. The following comments indicate that Negro policemen consistently find themselves denied the social recognition and respect of being police officers simply because they are Negroes.

> I'll give you some examples of this. My partner and I are on radio motor patrol duty. It's an ambulance call. When you arrive (and this example is in the Yorkville section of New York) you find a low income family of Irish background and the grandmother is hurt with a broken arm. We respond, my white partner and I, and the ambulance which has a white driver and a Negro attendant. The daughter and son-in-law are present at the scene. And the patrolmen are attempting to help her. She turns to the Negro patrolman and says to him, "Don't put your hands on me!" I can't touch her. Can you imagine that. I come to her aid, and she tells me to get my hands off her. (25)

> There is an emergency call. A nurse lived in the East 80's. Four radio cars respond. That means sixteen patrolmen.

There are fifteen white patrolmen and one Negro, me. My car caught the call, and my partner and I dash into the apartment. The woman is in a night gown. She is hysterical. But when she sees me she goes into complete shock! Ironically, I had to get all the information from her because we got the call. Things were running through my mind that the assailant was a Negro and this was why she responded to me, but he was white. She almost screamed again when she saw me. There I am with my brass buttons and my shield. It's obvious I'm a policeman but she goes back into shock. I keep telling her I'm a policeman. I actually ran downstairs and told my partner that I didn't want to have anything to do with the case. But I went back up. I have dozens of such incidents. (25)

The Negro policeman does not enjoy a tenable identity even among Negroes. While he may see the uniform as a badge of professionalism, signifying his escape from menial ghetto jobs, to some Negroes it is seen as the negative image of the representative of white society in their midst.

The problem of being called an Uncle Tom by the Negro population is the most negative feature. During the riots of last year I only hit one fellow. And I hit that fellow real good because he called me an Uncle Tom. I know that I shouldn't have done this. I lost my head and got emotional about this. I see it was wrong now but no Negro is going to call me an Uncle Tom because I wear a police uniform. (37)

THE UNIFORM AS A POLICE TARGET

The uniform can also be considered a target for the department. In this sense, the Negro policeman feels he is subject to criticism by the department, superiors, and white policemen when he is in uniform. It is probable that white policemen feel the same way.

179

In uniform you are a target for all the complaints that come from within the department. When you are out of uniform the bosses don't know who you are. Once in uniform you are pinpointed. The dream of every cop is to get out of the bag and into plainclothes. The civilian complaint is another thing. But the most serious complaints are from the department and every complaint is a point off advancement. (14)

This policeman went on to suggest racial discrimination by the department.

The Negro is subject to more complaints than white cops. I had fourteen complaints and then I stopped counting—plus seven transfers from one precinct to another. (14)

Another policeman made the same point when he talked about discrimination in promotions as the most negative feature facing him as a Negro policeman.

The fact that he can't assimilate himself in the police department as any group can. You are always first seen as a Negro. Therefore, anything that comes thereafter is based on personal preference. And this is the result of what people bring with them on this job. When they look at you or assess you, or relate to you, whatever the case may be, they look at you as a Negro. They always think what effect you being a Negro will have on the job. Say you are a plainclothesman in mid-Manhattan. The chances are very good that because you are a Negro you will not be considered for this job. The feeling is that you would be better in Harlem. The trouble is that the superior officer really has no basis for saying that you will be more effective in Harlem over, let us say, Manhattan. But, being a Negro is the information that is used by him in making such a decision, but without any basis in fact, as to why this should be so important in your effectiveness as a policeman. (34)

The following comment shows that the Negro policeman feels he is excluded from many specialized divisions in the department.

180

This exclusion prevents him from receiving the possible economic and social benefits associated with these more responsible police positions.

> Because you're a Negro you can't get into certain departments or divisions, like specialized departments: Detective Bureau, Homicide, Burglary, Pickpocket Squads. In these specialized departments it's who you know, not if you're qualified. (5)

One policeman felt that being Negro carried a unique form of stigma. More accurately, it is the attitude of the white policeman towards the Negro policeman that is unique.

> The most negative is the most obvious feature—is the physical characteristics. You can't hide what you are. If any prejudice exists in the department, you can't actually hide from it. The same applies to the Puerto Rican who is stuck with this name. So for the Negro the fact that he has color is the most negative thing. Not that I am ashamed of color, or any Negro is ashamed. It's just a fact that's all. A good example of that: when you see a person assigned coming into a precinct and he is colored, you can see the reaction in their faces. When you are just a name, you are just a name. I was the first colored sergeant in the ———— precinct. After the promotion your name goes on teletype and tells them where you are being assigned and your name. When you walk in they are surprised. This doesn't mean they are not cordial or courteous, but they can't hide their surprise. They never expected a Negro sergeant. The physical characteristic is the biggest shock of all. (21)

The Negro policeman, as we have tried to show, is in a status dilemma, holding contradictory self-images. The uniform he wears sets the conditions for the change and development of different relationships, new loyalties, different motivations appropriate to the position achieved, and a new identity. Yet at the same time he is a Negro with an identity of his own, the color of his skin defining and limiting him as such. Each horn of the identity dilemma (that is Negro–policeman), according to the social context in which he works, transforms itself into the other. Negroes respond to him as an agent of "white power" and constantly remind him of his being Negro. In a white area, and in the way he perceives his relationship to the department, he may be regarded simply in terms of his race. Under certain conditions the two identities are joined and do coexist.

Furthermore, we would observe that different role definitions are expressed by two different types of policemen: those policemen who consider the most negative features of police work to be the uniform itself, and those policemen who considered the negative features to arise from racial identity. The attempt is made by each type of policeman to resolve the dilemma by assuming one or the other identity through ways which seem most comfortable to them.

Lastly, the desire to get out of the uniform (a persistent theme throughout the discussion) is an attempt in practical terms to resolve the dilemma the Negro policeman faces. This desire to get out of the bag can be summarized by delineating the two kinds of rejection of the uniform expressed by these men.

1. Getting out of the uniform removes one from the vulnerability of police work, and is an attempt to dissociate oneself from the role conflict involved in being a Negro and a policeman concurrently. This is characterized by the Negro who rejects the authority as symbolized by the uniform.

2. Getting out of uniform gives the Negro policeman a form of social anonymity. This applies to both those Negro policemen who reject the authority and official identity of the uniform, and to those who reject the uniform because it symbolizes a low class of work. Thus, for both groups, rejecting the uniform removes one horn of the dilemma, the stigma of the uniform, and allows them hypothetically the luxury of receiving the economic rewards of police work without the negative social identity; in a sense "to have it both ways."

3. Getting out of uniform is a step up (a "mark up") from the "blues" to the white collar world of plainclothes. In addition, the work offers a higher salary range, more interesting work, and a position in which policemen can now potentially disregard the

formal regulations of the department that are binding upon uniformed patrolmen, or at least take the opportunity of acting more
informally in regard to police rules and regulations. This typifies
those policemen who rejected the uniform, since the uniform was
considered by them a symbol of working at the lowest level.

NONUNIFORMED POLICEMEN

Since being a Negro involves negative social esteem, the Negro
policeman out of uniform faces all the humiliations of being a
Negro, especially when he leaves the ghetto. If he is in uniform
he faces the negative images attached to being a policeman. Thus
while he most often dislikes the uniform, he does not escape by
removing his uniform. He merely transfers to another horn of the
dilemma. This has tragic consequences because the Negro out of
uniform may be subject to police brutality.

> There is no recognition out of uniform for the Negro and
> there is no respect in it. This is the dilemma of the Negro
> policeman. People are reluctant to believe that Negroes are
> policemen too, even with all your identification. Let me give
> you a couple of incidents that illustrate this to you. During
> the riots in Harlem, a young plainclothesman who was in the
> Narcotics Division was pushed by a white cop. He was
> pushed by this white cop and told to move on. The Negro cop
> told the white cop that he was on the job. The Negro cop
> tried to convince him and was about to show his identifica-
> tion when the white cop clubbed him—and the Negro cop
> could not fight back. He got clubbed so bad, you know how
> he talks now? He stammers—that's right, he stammers. If
> that was me, that cop would never have done that to me.
> I'm not just going to stand there and let him club me
> because he is a cop too. (8)

> In Harlem last year during the summer riots, there was a
> Negro detective who did identify himself but the white cops
> hit him anyway and told him they didn't care whether he was
> a detective or not, he was just a nigger to them. (34)

183

Such responses point to the fact that the Negro policeman can hardly exist without the uniform of one. Without the protection of the uniform this plainclothesman was responded to exclusively by his location in the configuration of social events, and by the color of his skin.

One of the above policemen related another incident that he was directly involved in.

> There was another incident that happened to me too. I was out of uniform one day and driving along and I saw a man that appeared to be messing around with a car as if he was trying to steal it. I stopped, went over to the guy and asked what was he doing. The white man got nasty and he refused to show me his registration or to tell me what he was doing with the car. The guy got more abusive and started to threaten me. So I had to put the billy upside his head. I took him to the station. The guy got three stitches and it was not until later did the guy identify himself as the owner of the car. Later when I went to the guy's house to talk to him, he still didn't want to believe that I was a cop. (8)

By responding to this white civilian with a strong assertion of his authority the Negro policeman placed himself. That is, this situation reinforced identification with the police role; one can only get by through dependence on one's police status.

Another policeman pointed to the fact that the Negro detective becomes a victim of his own color. White policemen may assume in certain circumstances that the Negro policeman out of uniform is the perpetrator of a crime. He is suspect simply because of his color.

> I have a fear (maybe I should call it a feeling) that when I am in a white neighborhood, and if I am by myself and making an arrest, I have a fear that some white cop will come up and shoot me! Because of the fact that I am not wearing a uniform which would identify me, the white cop might think I'm the one. It has happened you know. Last year in Harlem

184

> a Negro detective was beaten by white cops. You see, they
> would assume that being a Negro I was up to no good. If I
> am chasing a guy the chances are that a white cop will take
> a shot at me. And then it's too late to say I'm sorry. (33)

Consequently, another detective told of the importance of
looking like a policeman without the protection of a police uniform. He described the ways in which the Negro detective modi-
fies the arrangement of himself in order to link up with the environment. For without such modification the risks are great; life
itself is in danger.

> I have had problems with other detectives. There was a
> burglary in a white supermarket. Cops along the scene. We ar-
> rive a little later and we tell them who we are. The door is
> busted in and the cops are there. I arrive with a black coat on
> and I have my tam on (which I forgot to take off. In certain
> neighborhoods I wear it because it fits in, but in this neigh-
> borhood I forgot to take it off). One cop that I remembered
> meeting once comes up to me (he doesn't remember me)
> and says to me: Show me your shield. I tell him: Show me
> your shield. He actually thought I was the perpetrator and as-
> sumed this because I wasn't wearing a uniform and because I
> was a Negro. When I asked him to show me his shield, he
> realized that I must be a cop. And that was that . . . I also
> fear being shot by one of those white cops. This is a hazard
> being a Negro detective. You are taking a chance being out of
> uniform. So you try to look like a guy in uniform. You have a
> gun, a flashlight, and you wear a white shirt. These three
> things you use to identify you because you don't have a uni-
> form. Or you wait for white cops or go on the job with them.
> I don't go on prowler runs. That is too dangerous. The na-
> tural assumption that a white cop is going to make when he
> sees you is that you are a prowler. And under these circum-
> stances [prowler runs] you don't have a chance to identify
> yourself. So when you don't have the protection of the uni-
> form, you have to be real careful as I said—you wait for them
> holding your gun out so they can see it and telling them who
> you are, your precinct, or your name or badge number. Any-

thing that might make it clear to them who you are. But the risk is always there because they may not give you the opportunity and shoot first. Then it's all over. (34)

Indeed, the story about the plainclothes policeman in Harlem illustrates how ineffectual such modification can be. The risks for nonuniformed Negro policemen are great. For the identity of the Negro can change, not only according to his presentation of himself, but also according to the definitions held by those to whom he presents himself.

Other responses point to the failure of a Negro detective to register as such and account for additional problems of working out of uniform. The failure to make an impression as a detective is partly due to the stereotypes that Negroes and whites have of detectives in general. This forces the Negro detective, on occasion, to produce identification, which provokes feelings of humiliation. For example:

> At times you approach people being out of uniform and they disbelieve you are an officer at the moment . . . I think they think of a detective as being a member of the other race . . . And all of a sudden you tell them and they don't believe you. They ask for identification and you show them your shield, and that's not enough generally because they don't even believe you with that form of identification. Then they ask you for something else. Then you tell them you have a gun and you show them your gun. But that sometimes doesn't work either, not with me anyhow. We now have ID cards (an identification card with our pictures and corresponding shield number). But I refuse to show this. I don't think I should have to do this. It's kind of degrading to do this. I got to them in an orderly manner. This problem comes up primarily when you are conducting an investigation. (35)

Whites are especially unlikely to believe that a Negro can be a detective. They may phone in to the precinct to check on his identity after he has conducted an investigation, even though at the time of the investigation he has been given reason to believe that they have accepted his official status. If he is loitering about on a job, they may also phone in to the precinct complaining of a prowler in the neighborhood.

> Same problem. The problem of identifying yourself as being identified as this person. You have this conversation with a person. And you think this white person is going to go along with you. You leave your name and office number with this party. You find out later that this person has called the office to find out if you are what you said you are. They call the office to check and to see where the person's name they have is a detective. Also, in white neighborhoods people have made phone calls to the local precinct stating that two colored fellows have been parked in a location, and to ask the police to check who those people are. (35)

He also receives slight resistance from service personnel in luxury apartment houses, that a white detective would not face. The doormen and superintendents of these buildings may not cooperate with him, often expresssing condescension and hostility when he asks to see a tenant on official business. Frequently they ask him to use the service entrance even after they have begrudgingly accepted his identification.

> You have problems. More or less in better buildings. You get it mostly from the employees like the doorman and the superintendents of the buildings. And I found out that most of them had records or were drunks and they resented the fact that I was a detective. I would walk in and would tell them I wanted to see so-and-so and that I was a detective. Even after identifying myself they gave me a hard time. Sometimes they would tell me to take the service entrance before I identified myself. After identifying yourself, they would begrudgingly take you up after a lot of threats, arguments, and haggling. The people themselves are a lot of times surprised. Very seldom do they see a Negro detective on television. They are used to seeing the white cop. We always travel with partners. My partner is Puerto Rican who looks Italian. I would be stopped from going into the apartment even after

187

showing the shield. They just didn't believe that I was a Negro detective. People would say that they never saw a Negro
detective. (33)

The Negro policeman who is out of uniform is also placed into
a situation of being physically and psychologically dependent on
white police officers in making an arrest. The Negro detective in
this sense needs the white policeman for confirmation of a status
that *in fact* he occupies. To the extent that white policemen are
needed in making an arrest, the white policeman shares with the
Negro detective the rewards and citations that the department offers. The reverse is not true. Negro policemen thus believe that
Negro detectives do all the work, but white detectives get all the
credit. The following response illustrates this shifting of credit
to the white detective.

When I first came on the job we found it necessary to get a
white partner in order to be identified as police officers. I'll
tell you what I mean here. There were two colored, me and
another colored guy, and nobody wanted to believe us that we
were detectives. In this instance the neighborhood was predominantly Negro and Spanish. But it's also true for a white
neighborhood. It don't matter what kind of neighborhood
you work in. Now, when you actually are working you don't
want to be identified. So it's all right then. But when the time
comes where you want to be identified, the white detective
who has been in the background with you all along steps up
and then you are identified. See, they wouldn't believe us, so
when it comes to identify yourself, the white detective comes
up and says we are detectives. This is the point, where you
want to be identified for purposes of making an arrest, or for
the purposes of conducting an investigation, you need the
white detective in the background to come up and identify
you. (35)

Another Negro detective makes the point that because of his
color he is limited in the kinds of arrests he can make in white
areas. For example, he is limited in making direct collar arrests

(that is, when a prostitute solicits a policeman) on the grounds that the prostitute (Negro or white) will suspect that a Negro out of uniform, loitering about a street corner, must be a cop.

> When I was in plainclothes working with prostitutes, most of the arrests that I made were jump collars (when you follow them with another John). But it was hard to make a direct collar arrest (that's when the prostitute approaches you). This applied to both Negro and white prostitutes. In Harlem on the other hand if you are a Negro plainclothesman then you can make a direct collar arrest. But downtown the prostitute just picks up white men and consequently doesn't approach the Negro plainclothesman. Reasons for this: one, you are looking for the same thing they are; two, you don't have money to spend, or want a freebee (a free piece of ass); three, you want to shack up all night; four, or you might rough them up. Why not apply the same reasons in Harlem? Because when you are a Negro plainclothes downtown, and you are dressed up sharp, you are either a cop, a pimp, or a murphy man, playing the murphy game [a confidence racket]. The fact that you are Negro in a white neighborhood reduces the possibilities. The prostitute figures that you are either one of the three. She doesn't want a cop around her neck. She isn't interested in a pimp. She doesn't need a murphy man. So being a Negro reduces the kinds of arrests you can make. (6)

As the detective remarks, even if the prostitute does not suspect his official identity, her preference for white clientele who have money requires her to avoid Negroes whom she feels are not able to afford her services simply because they are Negroes. In either case, she will not approach a Negro detective with immoral intention, thereby depriving him of the opportunity of making a legal arrest.

This problem is given additional relevance when one considers the pressure to fill statistical arrest quotas working as a detective. Because of this pressure, the detective often finds it necessary to resort to dirty collar arrests, that is, needless arrests made for the sake of meeting arrest quotas which cannot be easily filled

189

through clean collar arrest procedures. And when these dirty collar arrest cases come before the courts, they are often dismissed for lack of evidence. In fact, they are considered illegal arrests. One police officer comments on the need to manufacture arrests when legal arrests are not visible.

> It's a rat race. The pressure is on to make a lot of arrests. And there are just so many clean collars out there. You can make other kinds of arrests that you wouldn't under other circumstances because of the pressure. You have to keep up an arrest record. And the higher you go up the ladder in the detectives the more arrests you have to make. And it gets harder and harder to make those clean collar arrests. Of course it depends on the area that you work in too. (14)

However, this is not the whole story. As we have seen, the Negro detective who works in a white area is often limited in clean collar, legal arrests. This is due to the fact that he is a Negro out of uniform, and therefore identified as a cop. Yet he cannot easily resort to dirty collar methods in making arrests against whites because of "political repercussions." Thus it follows that both the department and the Negro detective have interests in having Negroes work in Negro neighborhoods, where there are more arrests visible. More illegal, dirty collar arrests can be made there because lower-class Negroes have no "connections." One could conclude from this that social forces make demands for Negro detectives to work in ghetto areas, and to keep them there.

Being a Negro plainclothesman (or detective), also has advantages. The nonuniformed Negro policeman has the obvious advantage of color similarity and friendships, all translated into information not easily accessible to white policemen who work in Negro neighborhoods. This could be interpreted as giving him an identity (race) that the police department could use to advantage. At least, the police department makes use of his race and puts it to good use without the encumbrance of the uniform. Of course, there is also the advantage that detective work is a high level job and represents an element of mobility within the department. These advantages are perceived as such by the following

190

policeman, who indicated that because he is a Negro he can obtain information in a "discreet way."

> I prefer not working in a uniform. It's a help as far as our work is concerned. You can more easily work in an area in plainclothes and can obtain more information from persons in a discreet way. I couldn't work in uniform in Narcotics. Also, you feel you have advanced from being an ordinary person like the person walking the beat who is confined to a particular locale. (35)

Another detective made a similar point.

> A Negro detective is most useful in an area where they are dealing with a likeness—that is, working in a Negro area. It would be expected that the Negro would be far more proficient than the white in undercover work in a Negro area. (29)

The Negro detective may perceive advantages in working in white neighborhoods as well. One policeman suggested that his importance as a detective stems from the opportunity he has to make observations as a policeman without revealing his official identity, based on the fact that he is responded to as a Negro.

> I was working on a case and I am able to get in the neighborhood. I would put on an old coat and people would watch you as if you were going to steal something in a white neighborhood. And this would give me a greater opportunity to watch whatever I am watching. But I also had people call on me to a radio car that there was a strange man in the neighborhood. (33)

Nevertheless, the "strange man" in a white community, identified as a prowler of sorts, is not in any way inconsistent with the low social standing of the person as a Negro.

Although we generally consider stereotypes as isolating mechanisms, and debilitating to that person because it prevents him from having access to the necessary tools to break down racial barriers, the following detective shows that, on the contrary, a stereotype can be used as a police tool. It functions to get information from whites by playing on their prejudice and stereotypes of Negro workers. This means, ironically, that the Negroes' alienation from white society is used as a new principle of motivation, the use of information against whites. He commented:

> It is logical that Negroes who work in Negro areas as detectives or plainclothes are generally accepted by Negroes generally. Another thing, the Negro for the most part represents to the white community one who is prepared to perform menial tasks such as busboys, delivery boys, maids, nightwatchman, etc. Now Negro detectives working in various white places employed in these tasks for obtaining information that they could overhear would be at an advantage, because of the fact that whites would never assume that the Negro overhearing this conversation would use it against them. They never identify the Negro as a police officer or undercoverman because of their stereotype regarding the kinds of occupations that Negroes hold. Working on this stereotype, the Negro detective has been able to get information from white areas. (29).

He then went on to justify a discriminatory police policy of deploying Negro policemen to Negro ghettoes, by stating that Negro detectives would not be successful if they worked in white precincts.

> A Negro detective in a white community would be at a disadvantage normally because he doesn't have social contacts with whites, and because his motives would be either suspect or questioned on the part of the white community. If a Negro was to commit an assault and robbery at Tiffany's on Fifth Avenue and in escaping ran off Fifth Avenue, he would be the easiest one to apprehend because of being in an area generally where there would not be too many Negroes. Yet, of a similar crime perpetrated in a Negro neighborhood, his apprehension might not be too successful. And this is an

analogy that would easily apply to a Negro detective and the problems he would have working in a white area. Say for instance there is a crime syndicate operating. And it is necessary to infiltrate the syndicate. But the mere fact of using a Negro undercoverman to get into the syndicate (assuming the syndicate to be run by whites) would create the same situation as a Negro attempting to get in a white restaurant in the South. Even like undercoverman Wood.[1] The only reason he was successful was for the most part because the conspirators were Negro. If the conspirators were white, Wood would never have been taken into their confidence. (29)

This policeman illustrates that nonuniformed policemen are also used as undercovermen ("political spies"), and many of them work, such as Wood did, for the Police Department's Bureau of Special Services, a secret office of the police department.[2] In addition to its undercover work in subversive groups, this office has been described as offering "protection for visiting dignitaries, including the personal security of the President and Vice President, and keeps track of such developments as strikes and deportation proceedings."[3]

Another Negro undercoverman, Adolph Hart, who worked for the same office, was instrumental in infiltrating the Progressive Labor Party, and acted as an important witness for the prosecution in convicting William Epton, its vice chairman, whose indictment and trial grew out of his alleged activities during the Harlem riots of July, 1964.[4] Hart was reported to have said at the trial: "Epton had suggested that he [Hart] go upstate and learn to shoot and that the Progressive Labor Party would supply him weapons and ammunition."[5] And he was told by Epton that

[1] Raymond Wood, a thirty-one-year-old Negro rookie patrolman, was selected for undercover work to infiltrate the alleged pro-Castro terrorists who planned to dynamite the Statue of Liberty and other national monuments.

[2] *The New York Times*, February 17, 1965.

[3] *Ibid.*

[4] *The New York Post*, November 30, 1965.

[5] *Ibid.*

members of the group "will fight . . . and are ready to die for the Negro."[6]

Such undercover work naturally leads to strong words, particularly on the part of those individuals who have been subjected to the functions of that office. As William Epton pointed out at his trial:

> I can offer pity for Adolph Hart—pity as a human being, as a man, and, most of all, as a black man. In the history of mankind there have always been traitors and stool pigeons who have sold out their people for twenty pieces of gold, and, in his case, it was for less. I very well understand that he is a sick man. Who else but a sick man would swear allegiance to a government and a system that has enslaved his people, murdered and raped his women, attempts to poison the minds of our children and make them into the image of Adolph Harts? . . . One can see as a perfect example a Jewish person or policeman, living in Germany during the reign of terror against the Jewish people, whose function was to betray and inform on his people to the Nazis. But we know that history, and the people that make it, are the final judges of these modern day quislings. It makes me wonder about those people who have no friends except their fellow betrayers, who are not trusted by anyone . . . not even those who hire them. They are loathed by society and are probably held in disdain by their own families.[7]

However, to impute a quisling role to Negro undercoverman Adolph Hart as Bill Epton did merely points to the paradox that confronts the Negro nonuniformed policeman, and possibly as well to whites who are undercovermen. That is, the higher the Negro climbs in the police department in these appointed positions, the greater his secret grows as a policeman, the more he becomes an unknown menace to sectors of the Negro community, and the more he is reviled as a traitor. The quisling role is therefore a function of the Negro policeman's mobility within the

[6] *Ibid.*

[7] As reported in *We Accuse: Bill Epton Speaks to the Court,* Progressive Labor Party, February, 1966, no pagination.

department,[8] his sense of duty in fulfilling the functions of his office, and his color which allows him access to information.

Yet it should be made clear that not all Negroes feel this way about the undercover Negro police officer; and after all white criminals dislike policemen. In addition, the idea that the more he rises in the police bureaucracy the worse a Negro policeman is may be true only to the extent that Negroes think that the whites use police against them.

In conclusion, as a policeman the Negro is expected to carry out the functions of his professional role and to identify with the world of the police. The professional code, among other things, defines the department as a moral agent *sui generis,* whereas his own identity as a Negro, and his separateness and independence as an individual, are subordinated to the collective aims and functions of the department. To some extent, the department has succeeded in sharpening his identification with the collective life of "sacrifice" and duty. This could be considered satisfying, in principle, to those Negroes who want to lose their identities as Negroes. However, for doing so, they must now suffer the penalties of being identified as "cops," subject to the stigma identified with the uniform. For those men who define their role from the point of view of being Negroes and policemen, they must suffer the dilemma of their dual identities. Although being a Negro and a policeman are sometimes interconnected and interdependent, we have seen that under certain conditions the two statuses are in conflict with each other. In this latter sense, consciousness of being a Negro subjects the individual to being damned twice: once for being a "cop" and once for being a Negro.

It is the despised features of being black in blue and identified as such which set the conditions for becoming a nonuniformed policeman. The rejection of the official authority implied by the uniform, and the rejection of a uniform which symbolizes working at the lowest level, are the reasons for wanting to join the

[8] In this regard, Raymond Wood was given an on-the-spot promotion which entailed a raise from $6,325 to $8,126 a year, the respective scales for a rookie patrolman and a third-grade detective. *The New York Times,* February 17, 1965.

ranks of the chosen. But getting out of uniform, either by chang-ing clothes or by promotion, as a way of resolving the conflict of being a policeman, is now the price one pays for being a Negro. The Negro policeman must now contend with his own "invisi-bility" as a policeman. The price he pays can be summarized as follows:

1. When he wears civilian clothes the public refuses to believe he is a policeman. He is given no recognition precisely at the time when such recognition is needed, to identify himself as the holder of a police status. Consequently, he finds himself humil-iated in attempting to establish his official identity.

2. Even other personnel of the police department refuse to be-lieve him. Furthermore, this forces him, under certain conditions, to manage himself so as not to be identified as a perpetrator of a crime, and run the risk of being killed by other policemen. This risk keeps him away from prowler runs.

3. His anonymity as a policeman highlights his dependence on white policemen at the time of making an arrest and conducting an investigation. This means that white policemen are needed to confirm the Negro's identity as a policeman. While confirming his identity as a policeman, the white policeman indirectly af-firms his low prestige as a Negro. This is an expression of the ambiguousness of Negro authority. Further, this dependence forces him to share credit with white policemen, when white policemen only perform nominal duties. Since this arrangement is not reciprocal, the Negro policeman resents this exploitation by whites.

4. He is limited in the types of arrest he can make, which potentially puts him at a disadvantage in getting promoted in the detective hierarchy. In order to maintain his position as a de-tective, or conversely, to stay away from the uniform, he must maintain a high arrest record. However, his color acts to limit him in this regard if he works in white areas; consequently, he has a vested interest in working in Negro areas. Since he is forced to make a large number of arrests in Negro areas his behavior rein-forces the stereotype that he is an agent of the repressive white power structure.

196

5. The reaction to this role, especially as it conflicts with a race identity in civil rights demonstrations, intensifies his self-hatred.

6. His uniqueness as a Negro allows him access into the by-plays of the Negro community. However, while it helps to make his work in the ghetto effective, his role may establish his identity as a quisling in the eyes of his ethnic peers.

8

Conclusion

In a truly democratic society being a Negro and a policeman should create no special problems. The democratic ideal of equality would operate in such a manner that he would have equal opportunities with whites to enter the force and rise through the ranks, since it is a civil service office and the standards are presumed to be impersonal and objective. What is regarded today as a lowly, albeit important, role of societal regulation would be accorded its due prestige, which is not now allowed even to higher ranking white policemen.

We need not, however, postulate a utopia in which the regulatory and repressive functions of a police force are separated to realize that whatever the problems of the white policeman, the ones of his Negro counterpart are far more complex and tension-producing. Both external situations and psychological ambiguities

199

are associated with the Negro-cum-policeman role which society has dichotomized for him.

In discussing the many aspects of this role we have tried always to view the Negro policeman as both the actor and the acted upon. How does he see the department in terms of its official ideology and its actual functioning? Does he have a conception of the policeman's role and in what ways does it differ from his actual experience of it? What are the foci of the tensions for him and the Negro community—the white policeman, the department, the white political establishment, or the white citizen? This constant evocation of a double image has in itself helped to provide the framework of this exploration.

These contradictions and ambiguities are evidence of the fact that white society has not yet resolved the dilemma of racial superiority and democratic ideology. Historically, Negroes were not recruited into the force but discouraged from joining it. The role was reserved for white first and second generation immigrants who used it for purposes of occupational mobility. The character of many of the urban police forces is based on past processes of ethnic selection which have made the Negro policeman an *arriviste*, "pushing" his way into areas previously occupied by white minority groups. The decision to encourage Negroes to join the force was not simply an opening up of a new set of jobs on a universalistic basis. It was due, in part, to a shortage of white recruits, these lower-class groups having been acculturated and no longer available in sufficient numbers. Further, the decision to bring Negroes into the department was based on two political factors: the new consciousness of the Negroes' racial identity, and the swift rise in the proportion of Negroes living in the central city.

Bringing Negroes into the police force accomplished a number of desirable results for white political leaders. To offer relatively high-paying jobs to men in a community where unemployment is high, without adding to the cost of running the city, is indeed helpful. It was also thought that adding Negro police to the force at a time when racial tensions were high might help avoid clashes

200

with the Negro community and counter its hostility. Moreover, on technical grounds, it was recognized that Negro policemen, because of their color, could be far more effective in dealing with a ghetto population. He would know the inside, intimate structure at the block and neighborhood level as no white could. It was also hoped that Negro offenders would respond more passively to a Negro arresting officer than to a white. Were violence to ensue during an arrest, the onus of police brutality, real or imagined, would be removed from the department and the white community.

In other words, the Negro was hired, not because of greater freedom of opportunity, but because he was a Negro, as if one were to say to a colored actor that his parts were limited to servants and Othello. This set the stage for his being treated in many ways in terms of his racial identity, rather than his professional one.

Despite the racial factors involved in their recruitment, the bureaucratic, civil service structure of the police department rendered the job attractive to mobility-oriented young Negroes. The lack of opportunity in other areas enhanced the desirability of this one. It must be remembered withal, that as with other civil service positions—welfare investigator, teacher, and so forth—it allows Negroes with a fair education, ability, and energy, to reach levels not possible in other occupations.

Thus, most of the men interviewed for this study joined the department because of the civil service opportunities it provided, rather than having been attracted by the idea of being a policeman. They indicated that they were aware of the factor of race when they made their decision that civil service jobs provided them the best opportunities, particularly in view of the non-discriminatory regulations.

Once they had entered the department they were subject to the influence of occupational training which inculcated new habits of mind, and were presented with a new ideology which transformed their jobs from a mere set of opportunities to a series of demands for adaptation to a complex institution. They were

201

required to base their acts henceforth on their recently acquired identity; police training and pride in having achieved this new status inspired them to do a good, professional job.

There also seems to have been an attempt to make themselves more than just professionals. They have justified their choice of job by pointing out that they can help Negroes, especially Negro youth, by performing a necessary job with greater sympathy than a white policeman would be able to bring to it. Others rejected this humanitarian stance and merely pointed to the upward economic mobility they have achieved by becoming policemen. In terms of their new middle-class status, higher incomes, and relative security, they are far removed from the poverty of their youth and the deprived conditions in which their families may live even today. Judged by the standards of the Negro community, in which middle-class status is acquired far too infrequently, these policemen have come far. Many have attended college or the Police Academy and now have a degree of education still rare for the rest of the Negro community. Thus they have gained prestige in the eyes of their middle-class peers, and while wearing the uniform, a degree of respect is accorded them by at least some members of the middle-class Negro community.

However, these Negro policemen find that there are indeed drawbacks to being a member of the force. Since some of the more manipulative motives for recruiting them are understood by parts of their own community, they may be viewed as agents of an outside, repressive, discriminatory, or indeed anti-Negro, white society. Moreover, they are regarded in this fashion precisely by those lower-class segments of Negro society from which they have emerged, whose values, after all, they shared in the past. This makes them vulnerable to the charge of being Uncle Toms or Charlies, thus forcing them to examine their own consciences to discover the truth of the matter.

Today we are increasingly aware that in the Negro ghetto a vast segment of the population is unable to accept white middle-class standards of legality and criminal behavior, so that the Negro policeman is continuously put in a position where he must make arrests for acts which are not regarded as particularly criminal by that community. He is faced then by a number of alternatives, all of which are unpleasant. He may become a Javert, a legalist, one who makes his arrests compulsively. He may try to avoid those situations—policy operations, street gambling, drunkenness—in which he would be forced to make an arrest for actions his community considers noncriminal. When it comes to civil rights demonstrations his choice becomes excessively difficult. If he does not make the arrests considered necessary by police procedure, he is thereby rejecting part of his professional role. It may also be conjectured that even though he violates the departmental standards of a good cop, he may still not have gained any more respect of the Negro poor. His refusal to take action can be interpreted by them as his being too chicken, or "he's getting paid off."

The most pathetic descriptions of the typical situations encountered by the Negro policeman are those which show him as wanting to isolate himself from all his friends and neighbors to avoid being embarrassed by them or avoid embarrassing them. Friends and neighbors will avoid him because he might discover them involved in a situation which renders them liable to arrest, or they may see him as an alien white influence in the neighborhood.

In a similar fashion, he begins to despise his uniform which stigmatizes him in the ghetto as the agent of outside white society. But on the other hand this uniform is the symbol of his accomplishment in escaping the lower depths of the ghetto.

His professional status is endangered further by the attitude of offenders, particularly wild Negro youths, who are not professional criminals and therefore do not respect the professional status of the policeman. These youths will attempt to evoke his guilt feelings by trying to force him to be lenient because "you're one of us" or to con him into neglecting his official duties. At times, because of their hostility to whites and the white establishment of which the Negro policeman is a conspicuous symbol, they may try to provoke him into acting the role of the brutal sadist so as to justify their own rejection of the society which in their view has rejected them.

Whatever action he takes to resolve the dilemma, the guilt

associated with being a man who has "betrayed" his race is evoked. Whether he becomes a soft touch and thereby less than a professional, or a brutal Cossack, a hardliner making more arrests than necessary in order to defend his professional status or avoid being conned, he is still responding in terms of being a Negro rather than being a policeman.

Most of these men are aware of these dilemmas and are able to articulate them. An effort to sail the narrow channel between Scylla and Charybdis is made when the Negro policeman decides to become truly professional and respond to all situations in terms of purely legal requirements, disdaining sympathy, anger, or passion. This is not a solution either, since no matter how professionally he acts, the realization that a Negro policeman is primarily a Negro is impressed upon him both by the department and by his white colleagues.

The administration of the department enforces his image by giving him assignments primarily in Negro ghetto areas where he will deal with a Negro clientele. Full acceptance of his occupational equality would mean an equal opportunity to serve in neighborhoods in which his placement depended on factors other than race. Yet from the department's point of view this would deny the necessities for which he was originally recruited.

Then too, given the ethnic factor in the history of recruiting, the patterns of promotion reflect the history of ethnic acculturation. The Negro policeman has superiors of Irish, Italian, and Jewish descent, who have achieved these positions over long periods of time and through much effort, in many cases overcoming discrimination against themselves. The higher positions represent a form of validation of themselves as immigrants in the process of acculturation and mobility.

The appearance of the Negro in the police department constitutes a threat to at least middle-ranking police officials in two ways. First, the prior social position of the Negro results in the white policeman's regarding this invasion of Negroes into the ranks as resulting in a lowering of the social position of the white policeman at all levels. Secondly, the promotion of the Negro policeman to higher positions is felt as an encroachment on a preserve thought to belong to the white policeman.

In civilian life, the white policeman, his relatives and friends, generally live in areas adjacent to Negro ghettos. We would speculate that to the extent that racial friction exists within the department, it is a reflection of the tensions between these older ethnic groups (uneasy in their newly acquired status above that of the Negro) and the Negro ghetto resident. However, the bureaucratic and civil service regulations of the department which forbid discrimination and discourage personal animus based on race, operate to dampen racial tension.

The occupational ideology of the force works to make policemen accord each other recognition as professionals at least in minimal terms. This would be especially true of the Call 13 distress signal—"cop in trouble"—in which the necessity of coming to the aid of a fellow officer overrides all other considerations. An element which furthers occupational solidarity is the struggle against their common enemy, the criminal, and the realization that by their position as enforcers of the law, they are separate from another entity known as "the public." Therefore in most cases, the norms of racial etiquette are followed so that both Negro and white policemen avoid emotionally charged taboo areas relating to race. Finally, it is to the interests of the white policeman and the department that Negroes be members of the force because of their accessibility to information in Negro areas and their ability to handle Negro clientele. These factors all act in part to contribute to the recognition of each other as professionals and to the mitigation of personal tension.

While these bureaucratic and occupational norms tend to dampen the racial tensions between Negroes and whites, their presence ensures that they will be acted out in more subtle ways. For instance, Negro and white policemen do not share a social life in nonwork or extrawork situations. When on occasion they find themselves in such a situation, an attitude of embarrassment and subdued tension is likely to exist, particularly when white women are present. In such situations the Negro is forcibly reminded that he is a Negro. At best, today, this social equality is restricted to official occasions.

It is clear, however, that race factors are always present on the job. Department policy frequently dictates that white and Negro policemen be paired on the job. This is not a result of a policy of integration or equality but acts to protect the white policeman from having to take action by himself against Negro offenders. The Negro policeman is there to protect his white colleague and the department from charges of real or imagined brutality.

Both Negro and white policemen are well aware of this. Quite frequently the white policeman will maneuver the situation to make the Negro policeman take more than his share of aggressive action toward the Negro offender. This is often done as a sadistic device to embarrass the Negro policeman or make him prove that this newcomer to the department is a truly "tough cop." Because the white policeman represents an established group, he does not feel the same demands for risk taking and proof of courage to be encumbent upon him. The probability of injury or even death in extreme situations is thereby increased for the Negro policeman, who is forced to take greater risks to prove his bravery and loyalty.

The Negro policeman, while finding it more difficult to reap the rewards of his civil service status, must prove himself more than is necessary for his white colleagues. In a sense this is always the case with the *arriviste*, and Negro policemen are quite conscious of these unusual demands, feeling that in order to achieve equal treatment from their peers and the department, they must make unequal efforts and show unequal ability.

Perhaps in self-defense, Negro policemen tend to feel that their white counterparts are inferior as policemen simply because they are white. Faced with few of the barriers which Negroes meet in the general job market, the white who becomes a policeman does so because he is unable to become anything else, in the views of many of these men. While such a racial ideology enables the Negro policeman to defend himself psychologically against his white counterpart, it serves to indicate that he has little respect for his role of policeman. He is one only because he has no better choice.

When the Negro policeman works in white neighborhoods he can be constantly defined as a Negro in the most racist use of the term. White citizens may be fearful of the Negro policeman in uniform, and may wish to avoid having to deal with him, preferring his white partners. They may abuse him, and are likely to charge, if they are offenders, that the policeman has been unusually strict and is getting even because he is a Negro and they are white. He may then be subject to unusual provocation by white offenders and other members of the populace, and to the conflicts arising from this provocation. If he overreacts, he knows he may be subject to complaints and subsequent charges; furthermore, he cannot be sure that he is not responding as an Uncle Tom, and affirming neither his official responsibility nor his own manhood.

The advancement of the Negro policeman to the relatively desirable level of plainclothesman is an escape from the stigma of the uniform and the onus that recognition as a Negro policeman carries with it. Without the uniform he can presumably operate solely as an individual, yet the doffing of his uniform brings with it, once more, all the disadvantages of being a Negro in today's society. White civilians are likely to treat him as an intruder rather than an officer, or simply as a low-status Negro, particularly if he operates outside ghetto areas. People seeing him loitering about on a job may phone in complaints to the precinct about a suspicious person. He may even be subject to arrest and brutality by white policemen coming from precincts other than his own, should he be unsuccessful in immediately identifying himself.

The risk and danger inherent in such situations keeps him away from prowler runs. Moreover, in the role of plainclothesman, he finds that he needs a white policeman with him when he makes an arrest or conducts an investigation in white neighborhoods. This is so because often white, and sometimes Negro civilians do not believe he is a policeman if he is not wearing a uniform. This dependence on the white policeman to confirm his official status at the time of making arrests forces him to share arrest credit with him, when the white officer may have performed only nominal duties.

Among Negroes he must be prepared to expose himself to the kind of disrespect or outright violations of the law from which his uniform ordinarily protects him. Thus his occupational mobility places him in a number of physical and psychological dangers to which the less successful patrolman is not as subject. His promotion is at best a mixed blessing.

It is in the area of civil rights that the problems of being a Negro policeman are most intense. Here his identity must be sharply defined whether he is actively or passively involved in civil rights movements. Unfortunately over the past fifteen years these movements have been associated in part with riots, provocations, demonstrations, and the possibility of violence. As a result, in his official position, he faces members of his ethnic group across physical and legal barriers. He realizes that his presence in situations of incipient or overt violence is due to the fact that he too is a Negro, and that he will be required to shoulder the burden of suppressing movements with which he is basically in sympathy, even though he may object to the particular group in question or the form of action taken. If violence does erupt, he is placed in the position of using his physical power to repress his friends, neighbors, and ethnic peers. In such situations he is likely to be denounced as a fink or stooge, a humiliation in the presence of white policemen.

He is also aware that his behavior in a riot, should one develop, is subject to the scrutiny of his white colleagues. If he is less than zealous he offends not only his ethnic group, but also his conscience. The problem is most acute when his white occupational peers act in a provocative manner to Negro civilians and a situation arises in which he himself may have to act against his brethren.

The clearest illustration of these double role contradictions is the issue of the civilian review board. The Negro community viewed the board as a means of defending itself against alleged police brutality. For the white policeman, represented by the Patrolmen's Benevolent Association, the attack on the civilian review board was necessary as a defense of the occupational autonomy of the police against all interference, even the interference of their political superiors, the democratically elected officials of the society they represent.

The propaganda of the Patrolmen's Benevolent Association, which emphasized the danger on the streets, is alleged to have conveyed to the nation that there was a "black menace." Supporters of the board accused the P.B.A. of emphasizing the racial dimension of crime in the streets. The Black Guardians, the association of Negro policemen, while not wishing to disavow their occupational ties with their white colleagues, clearly rejected the discriminatory suggestions implied by some of the board's opponents, thereby affirming their solidarity with the Negro community. In so doing, they were aware of the fact that they were raising the spectre of Negro policemen as an organized group within the department, and inviting charges of disloyalty.

Those Negroes who were opposed to the Guardians boldly raising the issue had no disagreement of principle with them, but objected on the ground that reprisals might be directed against them. They were seemingly willing to accept the fact that white policemen of the P.B.A. were free to express their views as an organized group even when these views appeared to them to exemplify discrimination, but as yet the Negro policemen in this group did not feel free to arrogate these rights to themselves. Implicitly they were operating on the assumption that they could be integrated in the force and treated as equals as long as they held no important opinions which differed from those of their white colleagues. Were they to differ, they were no longer equal. One might infer from this that equality in this case is an illusion and that the inequality, which in fact did exist, was similar to that inherent in southern racial etiquette. The Negro policeman will be tolerated as long as he is not uppity, and does not claim the same rights available to white policemen.

While the presence of civil service regulations within the police department creates a basis for the Negro achieving a degree of integration greater than that which may exist in organizations run on less theoretically democratic lines, the *de facto* existence of racially discriminatory attitudes on the part of both the white policemen and large segments of the white community make the question one of some urgency for the Negro policeman. Negro-white tensions within society at large have resulted in a repudiation of many of the norms, including legal ones, of that society. Many have gone further and rejected white society *in toto.* As agents of this white power, thought by them to reinforce the discriminatory system they so bitterly denounce, Negro policemen become outcasts from their community, even when they respond favorably to civil rights issues.

Thus the Negro policeman is placed in a special category by the department, his white colleagues, white civilians, and the lower-class Negro community. He has received some of the economic rewards of his mobility but he has paid for them with this double marginality. The question might be raised as to whether the Negro policeman can ever become fully integrated until such time as the society itself is. Until then he perhaps will not be viewed as a policeman but as an unclassifiable hybrid agent, reflecting, in a series of shifting fractured images, the Negro race and discrimination.